RED HOT BLUE NIGHTS

RED HOT BLUE NIGHTS

Based on love and crime, where
romance give way to betrayal,
where life and death are friends.

Revealed through the narrative
of the most wonderful short
stories, and action felt story poems
depicting crime and romance.

TOUCHED BY THE WINDS

by

LeRoy Hewitt, Jr.

iUniverse, Inc.
New York Bloomington

Red Hot Blue Nights
Touched By The Winds

iUniverse books may be ordered through booksellers or by contacting:

iUniverse
1663 Liberty Drive
Bloomington, IN 47403
www.iuniverse.com
1-800-Authors (1-800-288-4677)

ISBN: 978-1-4502-4522-7 (pbk)
ISBN: 978-1-4502-4521-0 (ebk)

Printed in the United States of America

iUniverse rev. date: 9/7/10

ACKNOWLEDGEMENT

Thanking the Heavenly Father for all his wonderful blessings and all things made possible.

Acknowledging my entire family for their love and support, and thanking them for their lifetime of inspiration.

Acknowledging the publisher of this book and thanking the whole staff for their excellent work.

Giving a very gracious thanks to all of you who take the time to read this book, or any part of it. May you spread love across the world.

INTRODUCTION

"Red Hot Blue Nights," is the third book written by the author. His first book is entitled "Crime Love & Black Pearls, and the second is entitled "Mad Guns Till Romance."

This particular book, "Red Hot Blue Nights," is based on love and crime, where romance give way to betrayal, and life and death are friends. Whether fighting for survival or wealth.

It speaks to the course of action that is taken when choosing love over madness, and life over death. Revealed through the narratives of the most wonderful poctic short stories, and action felt story poems depicting crime and romance.

The contents of this rare book speaks the language of true feelings, and capture the imagination.

TABLE OF CONTENTS

DANCING WITH THE SUN

Dancing with the sun,
beneath the
tall sky.

Till the Polynesian
days go
drifting
by.

Listening to the sweet
sounds, till the
sun goes
down.

Then comes the
twilight, fading
into the
night.

Dancing with the
sun, till the
day is
done.

Through the Polynesian
nights, till the
break of
dawn.

Dancing under the
night sky, with
starlight
In our
eyes.
Twirling flames of
fire, till the
moon arise.

Sizzling golden light,
burns bright,
into the
night.

Making room,
for dancing
with the
moon.

On a tropical island,
there is fun, when
dancing with
The sun.

In the sands of the
seashore, till
the evening
comes.

When love is in full
bloom, we dance
beneath the
full moon.

Waiting the arriver
of the sun,
till the late
afternoon.

Wishing upon a
shooting star,
may it come
soon.

On a Polynesian
evening, so
warm and
pleasing.

Reflecting the magic
of love, from the
wonderful skies
above.

Dancing with the sun,
where music
reverberate
from the
sky.

Where song birds retrieve
their melodies, then
away they
fly.

Music echoes in
the wind,
till days
end.

When boats takes to
the sea, sailing
fancy free.

Islander birds whistle their
lovely tunes. Soon, we
will be dancing
with the
moon.

A PICTURE IN MY MIND

A picture is in my mind, of your
lovely face. Impressed upon
my memory, for the
rest of my
days.

Enshrined in the gallery of my
thoughts, framed in
my heart.

Adorned with yellow
and red ribbons
of sorts.

A portrait of yesterday,
with the smile that
light up your
eyes.

reflecting precious
moments, when
it was all blue
skies.

A picture in my mind, worth a
thousand words of
happiness, of
you I find.

my heart gaze upon it each
day, at sunset and
twilight time.

Reminiscence of the sweet
memories that glows
from your
face.

Reflecting the delightfulness
of your gentle
ways.

A picture you left behind, that echoes
wonderful perceptions,
in the archives of
my mind.

It burns itself into my
memory with a
Passionate
flair.

Detailing the moments when
we were a lovely
pair.

It nestles in the eyes of my
conscious, casting
memories upon
my heart.

Sweet memories that
will never
depart.

A picture in my mind,
unleashing the joy
I will always
find.

Perhaps not everyday,
but most of the
time.

"A Picture In
My Mind"

THE HOUSE OF CARDS

Up from the ashes comes "The House of Cards." Resurrected from the ruins, after torched and burned. By a man who came in from the night, looking to set things right. He cursed the sun, came in firing a gun.

Looking for the ones who made off with his hard earned money, when the night was done.

He came for a money return, but the cardsharps were nowhere to be found, he took action, burning the place down.

Sending a wave of satisfaction through citizens in the town, who didn't want the House of Cards around.

Old gloomy tales had left a stain, too many men had been dealt a dead man's hand. The horror of a bad luck draw, prying eyes had already saw.

As time passed on, the House of Cards was rebuilt better then ever, with colorful neon lights shining bright, glowing in the shadows of night.

Some people called it the house of bondage, where patrons are lured into a game, only to be dealt a losing hand. Yet they return time-and-time again, never to win.

Perhaps hypnotized, or mesmerized by a "Black Magic Woman," conjuring up spirits from hell, casting voodoo spells.

Men and women comes from miles around,
just to lay their money down.

The House of Cards, where you are greeted
by queens and kings.

Dancing girls enter the stage and begin to
sing, putting on a show, waving at the men
down below.

Where high rollers gambled hard, and
the stakes are large. Women come to play,
twenty-four hours a day.

The Black Magic Woman struts her stuff,
serving spiked drinks till you get enough.

Her lips are laced with the kiss of death. Her
eyes filled with deceit. A kiss from her, you
will surely sleep.

She calls herself "Lady Luck," moving about
with a snake draped over her shoulders,
extending down and beyond her arms. A
symbol of her good luck charm.

The House of Cards borders on the edge
of a wild river, that lies at the end of a trail
scattered with unidentified bones. it has
been said that no one should travel this river
along.

Call girls sashaying from room-to-room.
Swinging their hips, casting spells like flying
witches riding on a broom.

Blackjack, is played in the back. Less then twenty-one, you are done. Many men lives have be ruined, some disappeared never to return.

A fortune-teller is waiting to tell you the secret of winning. For one gold coin she looks into her crystal ball, but your eyes sees nothing at all. How long, before your money is gone?

Be careful of the backroom deals that goes down, and the strangers who comes to town.

Make the wrong move, you may be sleeping six feet beneath the ground.

Beware of the men who stands nearby, with a gun quicker then the eye.

when enticed roll the dice, or you might get sliced, by the wielding of a knife.

Be careful what you say, or where you go. The House of Cards is a dead man's casino.

Engaged in a game of chance, thrust into a foolish trance, the dealer reads your cards. Scamming your money right from the start.

Women winking their eyes, giving you a quick smile. Wasting your time, because true love is hard to find.

Hiding behind the doorman, or the big bruiser. Before long your money is gone, you are the loser.

Concocting ways to lure you into false
hope, with magic spells, whistles and bells.
Palming cards, and breaking hearts.

Putting you in a daze, whether holding a
king high diamond, or an ace of spade. The
House of Cards never pays.

Treating you extremely nice, exchanging
your drinks between the toss of the dice.

Serving you a magic portion, that sends you
reeling like the waves on the ocean.

You may think that you're the winner, but
you might not get out alive, under the
effects of a poisonous high.

Disappearing from the backdoor, that lead
from the kitchen to the ocean's floor.

The House of Cards, where you can have
your fortune told, receive a threat for the
hand you hold. where dreams die hard, and
dignity is ripped apart.

A backyard cemetery, where missing persons
have been buried. Men who journeyed from
far off places, men with unfamiliar faces.

No one knows your name, when you play
a losing game. No fortune and fame, when
holding a dead man's hand.

Taking part when the cards are marked.
Staying awake. Playing for high stakes.

Trying to take control, waiting for a good luck draw, or a good luck roll, Promising the devil your soul. A winning hand you seek, but prone to a losing streak.

This is the essence of the House of Cards. Whether you place a bet, or play a game of roulette. Darkness will befall the House of Cards before sunset.

Beware of the risks before you start. Old habits live long, and die hard.

"The House Of Cards"

BEYOND THE WATERFALL

Beyond the waterfall, hear the
Wilderness call. Shouting out to
The wild, the eagle, and the birds
Of high, roaming the sky.

The streams, the rivers, among
The forest trees. Where men
Have pondered, beyond
The waterfall yonder.

The spring fountains, that flows
From the snowy mountains.
Crystal clear, moisturizing
The atmosphere.

Beyond the waterfall, lies the
Sparkling lakes, where the
dawn awakes.

The early morning sunrise,
Blending an array of
Colors decorating the sky.

Rolling meadows, in the open
Outdoors. Green valleys where
The four winds blows.

The flowers with the red roses.
The beauty they exposes.
Beyond the waterfall, comes the
Steaming sounds of the night calls.

The gray owls and the nighthawks,
Whose eyes have seen it all.
The whirlpools, the seagulls
Taking a snooze.

Hear the call of the winds, echoing
Against the surrounding wall,
Bouncing of the waterfall.

Where the whooping cranes struts
Their stuff. The deer take leaps,
Bouncing through the pine bluffs.

Cedar trees stands at attention,
Displaying an array of evergreens,
Flaring with three dimension.

Where the birds builds their nest,
And the tone of their music
Sounds the best.

Beyond the waterfall, comes the
Birth of the sun. that spread
Across the days, where the
Sunset rays, goes to fade.

Where the green trees grow tall,
And the wild animals love to brawl.

" Beyond the Waterfall"

ONE LOVE

Our hearts are indulged in one love.
as fresh spring air. One
love we will
share.

One love, with a heart that's
not conceded. Is all
I ever needed.

Your love for me; my love for you.
A flower of one love, in the
hearts of
two.

Like a bright red rose, renewing it's
fragrance each season, as
it flourish and
grows.

One love, shinning bright within
our hearts. With the light
of a million
stars.

With kisses just for one.
Kisses of love, not
Just for fun.

Bearing tender feeling of affection.
With wings of true love,
moving in the right
direction.

That blossom with sweet memories,
and warm dreams
of serenity.

Sweet lyrics burned in the heart
of our love. Sparkling
as the countless
stars above.

One love, is what I've been living
for. Out of a dream, you
are my beauty
queen.

My awakening eyes,
have finally
seen.

One love, flying with wings of
doves. The birth of a
treasure, you are
my living
pleasure.

Giving warmth to my soul,
my heart will
never grow
cold.

One love, with a thousand kisses,
your love is what I've
been missing

"One Love"

PAPER DREAM

As I lay upon my bed, a "Paper
Dream" played within my head.
Lasting just a moment in time,
then drifting swiftly from my
mind.

floating on air, on a cold winter
day. Scattering in the winds,
then carried away.

Memories of you in the pages of
my mind, tossed and crumbled
then left behind.

Blowing in the wind, torn apart
till no end. Once seemingly
alive, but only a Paper Dream
trying to survive.

Paper Dream, took wings to fly,
like birds of the sky, when the
magic died.

Like an old song, and the
melody that fade with time,
Paper Dreams are burned from
the pages of my mind.

Paper Dreams that never last,
taken from the memory, cast
into the past.

Dwindling Paper Dream, as if
my eyes have never seen. Fading
images that once were sweet,
gone with the memories that's
obsolete.

Once showcasing distorted
pictures that swirled rapidly
in my imagination, leaving no
room for variation.

Gone is the thought of holding
hands, and the plans for new
romance. Only Paper Dreams
are left in the sands.

Gone are the silly notions that
my heart once drew, like an
eagle that came into view, then
away it flew.

Embellished with faded wishes
just days ago. residing in the
corner of my mind, for only a
moment in time.

Visions of you, back in my arms
again, once flowed through my
head like a stream, a distorted
scene, but it was only a "Paper
Dream."

THE FACE OF AN ANGEL

She had the face of an
angel, a total
stranger, when she
came to me.
Tender and sweet, she
turned out
to be.

She was bearing the
flames of love,
with stars in her eyes;
sunshine in her
smile.

She ignited a bright glow that
burns within
my heart. The burning love of
romance, for kisses
to enhance.

Enchanted love, brought down
from the
heavens above, on the wings
of an angel, once a
total strange.

Her love shined with a scarlet light,
that sparkled pretty and
bright. Her face lit up
the night.

Fresh flowers, for a fresh
face,
to her I gave. She brought
the flames of love,
to all my days.

"The Face of an Angel,"
once a total
stranger.

VAMPIRE NIGHT

The night was just getting started, from a day of play, I was just departing.

It was the night of the eclipse. The earth would cast its shadow upon the celestial moon. It was to occur sometime soon, cutting off the brilliant light, from the darkness of night.

Earlier that day, I rode my bike down through the forest to visit my Grandfather. It was his birthday. Just for a few hours, I had decided to stay.

He lived in the countryside. Where the blue sky stretched far, and wide. The kids next door, and I went out to play.

My name is DeVoy. During that time, I was just a young boy, of fifteen. Skinny and lean, I thought my mind was keen.

We played among the hills, across the green fields. In the countryside, running for miles, beneath the sunny sky.

Before I realized, the sun had gone down. Sunk into the twilight, making way for the night.

As we indulged in laughter and play, the night had came alive, spreading darkness across the countryside, at the end of a beautiful summer day.

"I must be getting along," I yelled. When I was about to head for home.

"Hey! Aren't you afraid?" asked one of the girls, with whom I played.
"It is Vampire Night," she said. "Haven't you heard? The earth is going to cast its shadow upon the moon tonight, cutting off the light." she yelled.

"No, I am not afraid." I replied. "There is no such thing as Vampire Night. There will be plenty of light, coming from the moon. Besides, I will be home soon."

I grabbed my bike from the ground. Swirled around, for home I was bound. "No, I am not afraid." Down the darken road I fled. Constantly telling myself that I was not afraid, over-and-over again, riding fast into the wind.

The full moon was hanging high. The earth cast its shadow upon the moon, and across the sky. Holding back the light from my eyes.

I was moving fast, making my bike rip, beneath the solar eclipse.

In an instant, the moon came out to the night sky, reflecting blue light before my eyes.

I continue to ride my bike exceedingly fast. Through the weeds, and through the grass. Riding by the tall trees, that aligned the winding path.

I came upon a tall wooden bridge. I went atop, and began to proceed across. Briefly I came to a stopped.

I notice a man with long shaggy hair, that hung down his back. He was a tall thin man dressed in black. He stood near a lake, my eyes began to search for another path to take.

As I forged along, I could see that he was eating something drenched in blood, from the palms of his hands.

It struck me as something out of the ordinary. Nearby, his eyes gazed upon a cemetery.

As I went passed, my eyes could plainly see a woman stretched across the green grass, laying near his feet. She was dressed in white. Beneath a glow of blue light.

I watched the man from behind a nearby tree. I was afraid to leave, it was I, his eyes might see.

He appeared to be very strange. He kneeled down over the woman, then began to nibble on her neck; with his tongue he stroked her face, at a very fast pace. Motionless she laid.

My eyes could see that he was sucking her blood. This was the behavior of a Vampire. So I had heard.

The strange man reached down, grabbed
the woman with his large arms, picking her
up; carrying her down to the lake. There! he
thrust her helpless body into the waters.

My hands began to shake. I then realized
that she was dead. I became extremely
afraid. I tried to hid, I was petrified.

My stomach started to ache. My whole body
trembled in fear. If he had laid eyes on me,
I would have had only seconds to live, I
would have been killed.

He quickly turned, staring in my direction.
He had now seen me, our eyes had made a
connection. All it took, was his deadly look.
Astride my bike, I rode fast into the night.
He ran after me, across the rocks, and
rugged terrain. The strange man came.

The front wheel of my bike hit a rock. I was
hurled into the air, thrown hard onto the
ground, paining in despair. My eyesight,
blinded by the glare of blue light.

As he came, he howled like a wolf. I picked
myself up, and ran as fast as I could. Straight
into the darken woods.

It was like an entrance to hell. I had injured
a leg when I felled.

I hopper away, and hid behind trees, among
thick weeds. He searched for me in and out,
running and wandering about.

My body lingered in pain, quivering
with fear. I had witness this man dump a
woman's body into the lake. Now it was I,
he sought to kill.

I was deeply disturbed. He wandered closer
into my sight. I could clearly see, that he
was the father of the kids in which I played.
When visiting my Grandfather, blazing the
summer days.

His name was Franklin McAfree. I had
heard others refer to him as the Vampire
Man.

Earlier that day I played with his kids. Now
from their father, I hid. Trying to escape the
wrath of this soul, that the darkness of his
heart must hold.

I was stunned, McAfree was now very
strange. He certainly did not look the same,
as he came. He appeared to be a different
man.

His eyes bulged outward from his huge
head. His face looked like something that
climbed out from among that dead.

When he hoar, I could see that his teeth
were like that of wolves. Growling on the
prowl.

On his feet, he was unsteady. His clothes
were ragged and bloody. His face was wet,
dripping with sweat. His eyes were beaming
red.

He was running through the field of
the dead. Diehard scary, creeping in the
cemetery.

Carcasses of wild animals laid nearby. A
strong odor was lacing the air, that brought
water to my eyes.

The Vampire Man leaned backward with his
mouth open wide. Howling with the wolves,
that echoed throughout the dark woods.
Sending terror across the night, running in
the blue light.

Blood trickled from his large wet lips, and
from his long hairy fingertips

I moved on with urgency, hoping that
his eyes would not find me. I pressed on,
looking for a way to escape.

Perhaps through the winding roads, or
maybe swim across the black waters to the
other side of the lake.

I was running hard in a daze. Through the
black mud, and upon brick walkways. With
distress etched on my face.

The Vampire Man, grabbed my bike. Flung
it into the night. Thrusting the bike into a
tree. Breaking it in pieces. In a rage, so was
he.

Suddenly! There he was, standing right
before my eyes. I continued to hid. I did not
believe in vampires, but what could he be?
He resembled the vampire characters, that I
saw on TV.

I asked myself, was he a man gone mad? or maybe he just dressed up in a Halloween custom, and his evil mind, never allowed his true identity, to resume.

Maybe, Masquerading, and misbehaving with his strange mind fading.

I came upon a pig farm where wild hogs roamed about. Digging in the ground with their snouts.

I hid among the swine, in an overgrown pasture. Crawling around, down near their bellies making myself hard to find.

I watched as the Vampire Man grabbed one of the men, who was herding the swine.

With a hard sweeping blow, he snapped his neck. Ripped it open with the swipe of his paw. Drunk his blood, and flung his body back into the herd.

Right then, and there, I almost fainted. Suddenly I sneezed, as the herd of swine trampled over dust and weeds.

I hung in there for a spell, my nose could not put up with that smell.

The Vampire Man heard my sneeze. He stormed in my direction through the tall trees. I could see him bailing through the high grass, moving very fast. I once again start to run, for my life I was concerned.

The herd of swine began to squeal and scatter. Upon the hogs I could see his shadow.

Swiftly he followed. Through the woods he was prowling, like a hungry wolf he was howling.

Fast he came, the Vampire Man. With his huge cold hands he took hold on me. "I got you now!" he said.

He grabbed me by the neck. His hands was rough and wet, hard to the bone, like a solid stone.

For me it was a night of hell. I tried to yell, struggling to get away. Words my lips would not say. It was as something out of a nightmare, the stench of death penetrated the air.

I wrestled with him, twisting and turning trying to break his grip. Upon my face warm blood spattered, trickling from his bleeding lips.

"Get your hands off me," I managed to say. "Turn me a loose." I yelled. It appeared that he was in a warlock spell. "let me go, I have been gone too long, I must be getting home." I cried out in a loud voice, I had not a choice.

"Who are you? Why are you doing this? Are you going to kill me," I asked. He said not a word, as we struggled in the mud.

It has been said, that the Vampire Man, and
his wife practices black magic. To suck your
blood, they would cut you with a knife, or
ripped open your neck with a violent bite.

Indulging in witchcraft. Living under a
voodoo spell, speaking to evil spirits from
hell.

The Vampire man was powerful and strong.
I was exhausted, my energy was gone.

He dragged my tired body through the
muddy waters. Pick me up; slamming
my body hard to the ground, making a
thundering sound.

My dazed eyes could see stars; my head
seemed to revolve.

Like a sack of potatoes stretched across his
huge shoulders, he carried me back to the
cemetery, where the dead was buried.

The thick fog rolled in from the shimmering
lake. I was out cold, then my eyes began to
awake.

I could feel his hot breath, breathing down
my neck. He seemed to be a total wreck.

The electricity in his body gave me a jolt,
then he grabbed my throat. As I struggled,
and fought.

His mouth open wide, I thought I was about
to die. Perhaps he would sink his long sharp
fangs into my veins, and suck my blood dry. I
was terrified, tears began to roll from my eyes.

With my free hand I reached down, to the ground. Grabbed a hand full of dirt. Then hurled a fist full of graveyard dust into his big red eyes, so he could not see. I managed to break free.

My legs needed rest, but I could not spare one moment. This man was obsessed, I could smell the scent of alcohol on his breath. Again I started to run, as fast, as my legs would turn.

I hid in back of an old log cabin, stooped behind the walls. He gave out a call. "Hey boy, where are you? Come on out now. I won't hurt you. Don't be afraid," is what he said.

"Did you have fun playing with my kids today." I could hear him say.

I ran near an old well, he followed closely on my trail. In an instant he dove for me; I ducked. He slipped and fell, falling into the deep dark well.

I escaped his sight, running through the blue light, out of the darkness of Vampire Night. The fog had gone. I struggled to get home.

The air rang out with the cry of black crows, as they flew wildly above the wilderness, with wings spread across the winding road.

My energy was spent; my mind had went
into descend. I was done; my legs ceased
to run. The fog that had set in, was soon
carried away by the wind.

McAfree, kept this part of his life concealed.
He was infected with wicked vampire skills.
Killing inside of darkness, and in the fields.

Nevertheless, the Vampire Man, managed
to climb out of the deep dark well, where he
had fell.

Finally I arrived home. My Brother drove
me to the police station where I filed a
report, on my own.

The Vampire Man was picked up by the
cops, leaving behind a trail of gruesome
murders, before he was caught.

The last I heard, he was convicted for the
murders, and other serious crimes, and
given a life sentence doing hard time.

It has been reported that Mcafree escaped
from the penitentiary. Scaling a high prison
wall, going over a barbed wire fence, when
he heard his wife call.

He was last seen roaming the wilderness.
Looking for someone to kill, using his
vampire skills. Living under a voodoo spell,
communicating with evil spirits from hell.

For awhile I was living in a nightmare, with
grueling images that were hard to bear.

I have managed to put all of that behind;
now I'm doing fine; living in a different
time.

I never go out on Vampire Night. To avoid
the fright, I sleep with a light. Only once in
awhile, do I recall that gruesome sight.

"The Vampire Night"

STRANGERS IN LOVE

I never knew anyone like you.
Who stole my heart
at first
view.

The first time I saw your face,
my heart beat at
fast pace.

A stare, and then a smile.
strangers in love
with gazing eyes,
just for a
while.

I could feel the vibes of
your love flowing
into my
heart.

Settling in my mind
for the very
first time.

Strangers in love, extending
an olive branch
of a dove.

I said hello, you said hi.
then sparks
began to
fly.

The magic of love
was in our
eyes.

In a moment our world
turned to blue
skies.

When we first met, it was like
the moon, and the stars
greeting the
sunset.

Visions of love lands,
dreams of
romance.

Notions of we two
strolling in the
sands.

Two hearts growing
as one, rising like
the morning
sun.

Strangers in love,
gifted by the
heavens
above.

echoing only in memory,
a birth of design.
Love that is
hard to
find.

Lasting just a
moment in
time.

Touching our hearts
within, then
vanish like
the wind.

An instant delight,
falling in love
at first
sight.

Hearts singing of love.
Composed in a
lovely
key.

Making beautiful music
blooming with
harmony.

"Strangers in Love"

LIFE IS MUSIC LIFE IS SONG

Life is music, life is song.
Lyrics of love, blending
With the stars above.

Like a dream, so it seems.
When magic is in the
air.
When love is everywhere.

When the sun is upon
Your face. Music thrives
In the summer days.

Sunrise blue skies bouncing
Of the ocean, with waves
Of devotion.

Beautiful lyrics, beautiful
Song. Life is fill with music,
When love tags along.

The blooming of spring flowers,
The music of rain showers.
The flamingo shows,
And the sounds of soul.

Golden rays of sunshine
Dancing past an afternoon.
Blue Jays whistling a tune,
Waiting for the rhythm of the moon.

The early morning sunrise
Melts away, sending music
Into the distant day.

Feel the music
Of life as it spins,
So goes the winds.

The pyramid of the sunset
Is a picture of song. Creating
Melody for the night to
Follow along.

The gentle winds harmonize
With the cool breeze, blowing
Summer songs with ease.

The soft rain, that taps upon
My windowpanes. Keeping in
Rhythm with spring showers
As the music empowers.

The gracefulness of the swan,
Swimming after dawn.
In a lake, or a beautiful pond.

The peacock with music in it's long
bright tail. Spreading colors of
the rainbow. Making music
with the magic of an echo.

A dazzling display of stars.
Sailing across the night sky.
Making music for the eyes.

Drawn by a love song,
Dancing where the
Moon once hung.

"Life is music
Life is song"

RAMPAGE

Rampage, one man driven to rage. A mind destroyed, never a reward. Violent assaults, trouble is what he brought.

Drunken on alcohol, someone placed a 911 call. Distorted senses, led to bad consequences. Filtering down to a police chase, charged in a murder case.

A shooting expedition. On the road to a deadly collision.

Wielding guns in hand. Living in vain, his troubles will remain, only to go down in flame.

Onlookers lines the streets. Fear and tension runs deep. People moving back, geared for a swift attack.

Rampage, trying to turn the page. Nightmares, and misery occupied his mind for days.

Bad writing on the wall, bears no secrets at all. His life will take a turn, then his soul will fall.

His life is now a waste. Like the blood that drains down his face.

Rampage, reflecting the guilt, ingrained in the human race. Robbing men of their faith, leaving not a trace.

Like the sand, whisking through an hourglass, his life will not last. The end will come swift and fast.

SWAT Team! The killing machine, arrives on the scene, instilled to be deadly, and mean.

Ready for a quick strike, with a shot that's exact. No prisoners will be taken back.

A mother shedding tears. Cops lurking behind shields, taking direct aim with weapons to kill.

A helicopter flying beneath the sky. Recording the scene with a camera lens eye. News crews standing by, waiting for someone to die.

Rampage, living in the last days. Evil men concealing their guns, passing laws, for the right to shoot anyone.

People trying to run, from the automatic machine guns. Blazing in the afternoon, until the low rising moon. Hostages are taken, lives are forsaken.

Rampage, a man living out his raging ways, with his blood he pays.

Gone insane, his heart is in pain. On a shooting spree. Struggling to fight back, against the police strikes, but refuses to flee.

Blasting non-stoppable rounds, soon he will go down. Carrying out a hard rampage, trying to deal with his blood thirsty rage.

Men run and hide. Women scream and cry.
No one want to die.

A policeman is shot down, by a blazing
machine gun rounds. To a cold grave the
perpetrator is bound, no way to escape, no
superman's cape.

Making plans, shouting out demands.
Waiting for a helicopter to take him high.
To a refuge across the sky.
His heart is trapped between love, hate, and
fear. Nothing on his mind, only shoot to
kill.

Soon he will be living in a prison cell, or
going down to hell.

Police snipers, with automatic rifles. Got
him in their sight. Time to pay the pied
piper.

Rampage, evil ways, no more sunny days.
Fire and smoke, rising in a haze. Gunned
down, by machine gun rounds.

The perpetrator was living hard, now his
grave is marked. His body lays cold, bearing
deadly scars.

High drama fads in the end. Smoke rises,
and spread within the winds.

His heart was in doubt, no way to escape.
No way out.

"Rampage"

WINTER WIND

Oh, winter wind,
where have you
been. You left at
autumn's
end. Now you are
back again.

Whistling cold,
sending chills
down to my soul,
the winter wind
blows.

Freezing my inner
side hard
as stones. Deep
down
to my bones.

Migrating before
the birth of
spring. Lingering
long
enough to hear
the
freshness of
spring, begin
to sing.

Reverberating
throughout the
season, for all the
winter reasons.

Echoing across
the mountain
tops, blowing
among
the frozen
raindrops.

Cold edges of the
winter winds, left
behind near the
month of may.

Bringing fresh
ocean air,
to a hot summer
day.
Swirling through
the frozen rain,
wild as a beast
that's
untamed.
Blowing
across the winter
plains.

Feeding off the
ocean blue,
so the winter
winds
swirled and
blew.

Riding on
the waves,
crisscrossing the
winter days.

Passing through
the sea, keeping
the blue waters
cold,
as they ought
to be.

Icing the black
lagoons,
swirling beneath
the
cold moon.

Fiercely blowing
through
the forest trees,
sweeping away
all the fallen
leaves.

Like a predator
gobbling up
the warm air.
Leaving
behind none
to spare.

Howling in the
night.
Blowing with
all it's might.
Covering
footprints with
sand.
In places where
we once ran.

Casting cold
shadows upon
the sun. Blowing
fiercely
before the winter
is done.

Winter winds,
whispering
in. From cold
snowy
mountain yonder
twins. Billowing
around the
bends.

Followed by
a scene of
evergreens.
Cascading
above and below
the mountainside.

Where the cold
rivers flow,
beneath the cold
winter sky.

Despite the cold
winter winds.
Wild geese and
migrating
ducks continue
to fly in.

Despite the
winter chills,
that whistle across
the open
fields.

My soul love the
way,
it makes
me feel.

Invisible to the
eye,
as it passes
by.

Blowing scattered
flowers in the
rain showers,
across the
cold winter
hours.

Winter winds, where
have you been.
Glad to
have
you
back
again.

MY HEAVENLY FATHER

My eyes would not see, my ears could not hear. If not for "My Heavenly Father."

The creator of the world, of every man, woman, boy, and girl.

He let's my whole life rest in the palm of his hand. My past, present, and future. He has the right plan.

He possess all power, glory, and might. If not for him in my life, I could do nothing. He gave himself for a sacrifice.

In times of need, it is he in whom I plead. He makes a way for my soul to succeed.

Through the power of pray, my troubles vanish in thin air. In him my heart is resting, reaping the benefits of all his blessings.

He touches me at the morning's dawn. To awaken my eyes, to the morning sun.

On the outside, I gaze into the sky. Giving thanks, for a beautiful sunrise.

He lay me down for
slumber in the
dark of night. Comfort my
weary eyes,
with a soft glow of light.

From the moon, and the
stars reflecting from a heavenly
sight.

I don't have the riches of
silver and gold, for this kind of
blessing I was not chose.

A brilliant mind I cannot
claim, but for the joy of life he
called my name.

In my walk with him I
failed to follow a straight line.
Felled short of his glory in the
test of time.

Yet upon my soul, his light
continue to shine, within my
heart, and within my mind.

"My Heavenly Father"

RED SKIES

"Red Skies," comes alive, with
Vibrant color. A beautiful
Display, on the evening
Of a cool summer day.

Skies of gold, reveals the
Wonder that unfolds. Blue winds,
comes rolling in. Across the desert
trail, seeming never to fail.

Sunrays, piercing the summer
Days. Reflecting upon the red sky,
Spanning for miles. Creating a golden
Scenery, bringing magic to the eyes.

Red Skies, white clouds crystallized,
Drifting by. A dazzling display,
Comes alive in a spectacular way.

On a grand scale, the view is
Breathtaking, from a mountain
Trail. The scenery is delightful,
The excitement is priceless.

Red Skies, standing by. Echoes
Colors of fire. A remarkable view,
Magnified after the fresh morning dew.

It stretches throughout the
Coolness of a summer evening,
When the air is fresh, and pleasing.

Painted by the sunrays, with
Colors from the milky ways.

Caravans moves along
Winding roads. Traveling
Beneath the skies of gold.

Red Skies, a hint that the day
Was about to slip by.

Fields of wild flowers, strung
Along the spring fountains. Inlaid
beneath the towering mountains.

A crystal clear waterfall,
Flows down a mountain trail.
A man stands near, holding
A silver pail.

The Red Skies, drew sky watchers
Out in droves. Lining the side
Of the winding road. Beaming
Eyes, on the golden sky.

We gazed upon the red sky,
Down by the seaside. The day
We rode by. Returning again,
From relaxing places, where
We had been.

Red Skies, harmonized before our
Eyes, with a golden sunset. Still
the show was not complete yet.

Where the evening sun melts
Away, out of the coolness of
A day. Into the night air,
With a glowing flare.

Fading yonder, behind the
Mountain bends, at day's end.
As a trend, it will return again,
With the changing winds.

Looming far and wide, awakening
The curiosity of a child. Birds flying
high, with pride, beneath the golden skies.

"Red Skies"
bring magic to my eyes.

STRAY CAT

She lived her life liken to a “Stray Cat.”
playing the part, migrating into my
heart.

With eyes of a feline, just strolling
through time. A unique breed, doing as
she please.

She runs with swindles and thieves,
where men are setup to bleed. A feline
queen, destined to succeed.

pacing the streets. Prowls along the
hillsides, with a deadly look in her eyes.
Stalking her prey, as she wander through
the day.

Enchanted feline eyes, in touch with the
stars that trails across the sky. She roam
along the city streets, where fire and
light, gleams in the night.

Where smoke rises from burned out
places, leaving behind crime infested
traces.

She charmed her way into my life, to
soft music from the ocean winds. Never
revealing the secret places, for whence
she had been.

My love for her was as a jewel, a
precious stone, but to me she did not
belong.

Drawn to her by the beauty that lain in
her face. The excitement she brought to
my days. Even in the cold, the beauty of
a flower must unfold.

She came to me from the world outside,
flashing her feline eyes, cuddling by my
side.

A picture of perfect light, that lit up my
life, but
when the stars came out, she went
prowling in the night.

Her way of life seemed to be sweet,
dripping with honey, but she was
cunning. Playing the roll of a gentle pet,
since the day we met.

Lady feline, for a moment in time,
played with my mind. Straying into my
arms, zapping my power to resist her
charm.

Persuading me to believe, in a heart that
is prone
to deceive.

The sunshine of my heart would soon
disappear. A bad moon was rising in my
atmosphere.

From my eyes she would holdback
my brightest light. Only her deepest
darkness would rule over my nights.

Stray Cat, dealing from the bottom
of the deck. Clawing her way into my
heart, exposing the wildcard.

Telling lies, with tears in her eyes.
Playing the game of love, faking
a winning hand, expecting me to
understand.

Into her face, agony and disgrace begin
to show. In
the game of love, you must reap what
you sow.

Drawn to a love that has been made
sweet by false hope, that would soon
vanish like smoke.

The sweet taste of nightlife, is not
without a hefty price. She is a different
breed, with unique ways to deceive.

Constantly looking for a place to stray,
letting nothing get in her way.

Eating fast food, wearing high heels
shoes, prowling in the night, heating up
the day.

In the season of true love she
procrastinated, spending excessive time
being intoxicated.

Once a ray of sunshine, now roaming
the streets looking for a dime, living in
the hollow of time.

Lost in her own shadow, where nothing
seems to matter.

Like an empty cloud that rolls in. Then
carried away by a strong wind.

Beware of the Stray Cat, living her life
like someone's pet.

Being slick and sly, casting deadly love
spells, with her feline eyes. Reflecting
blinding light, to confuse your nights.

Take a stroll, down feline road. Soon
you will be living outside in the cold.

"Stray Cat"
wearing different hats

GRAND THEFT AUTO

"Grand Theft Auto," a party where no man wants to go, but it's the only thing I know.

When I was seventeen I graduated from high school, despite braking all the rules, so I was accused. The way of life I had no clues.

I searched for a job, but did not find one. I hit the road, wild and bold. Moved to the west coast, to a city I chose.

Fell in with the wrong crew, got into trouble. They taught me bad things, things I never knew.

I was introduced to the game of carjacking. Started putting in work, carrying out my duties. That's when I was stabbed and beaten. I took a shellacking, weapons of choice I begun packing.

I had a craving for expensive things, glittering gold, and diamond rings. Black pearls, beautiful girls inside my world.

I begin living on an ambitious high, not concern whether I live, or whether I die. I was confused, had been abused.

Nearly shot down, by a police gun round. They think I'm just a clown, living on the wrong side of town.

With plans of my own, I started a business that I knew was wrong. I had no one to care for me, I didn't even have a home.

Places were setup for me to rob, it was my job, but I didn't like being involved.

Before long I went back to boosting cars, that's when the money started to roll in. I had run-ins with the law, but I learned how to win. Doing the same old things, time-and-time again.

I found my way into the underworld. I was given a jobs, paid big money for fancy cars.

I received instructions to lay low, listen to the satellite radio, and wait for the word go.

Gathering information from a system of high quality tracking, sponsored by men with big money backing.

From city-to-city I roamed. boosting cars, making bail, when I was thrown in jail, never staying in one place too long.

Roaming the streets, in cities that never sleep. Where the neon lights are bright. Where hustlers and con men go to sell their hype.

Fast talkers and streetwalkers are rampant, getting into fights, scamming money in the night.

Grand Theft Auto, constantly on the
go. to places like L.A., New York, and
Chicago. Towns that have no name,
spread out across the plains.

Driving long and hard. down crowded
streets, rugged roads, and freeways.
Behind the wheel of a fancy car for days,
going to places where the underworld
plays.

Avoiding the cops, making ten-grand a
pop. rolling fast and hot.

They tried to slow my roll, showing no
mercy for my soul. Pumping gun rounds,
trying to lay my body down.

The ray from the helicopter light, beamed
upon the night. No one knew my name,
just a man without a face. I was gone
without a trace.

Driving across the treacherous landscapes,
in the heat of day, in a quest to get away.
The cops were out to make me pay.

Squealing wheels, I was about to be killed,
but I have no fear. Something must be
wrong in my head. I'm thankful to be
alive, I could be dead.

I fell into a bad routine, hooked up with
an underworld scheme.

The bitter taste of poverty have driven
me insane. I must be a deranged man,
careening down the freeways with a gun
in my hand.

There was a time when my automobile was riddled with bullets. It begin to lose power, I had been fleeing for hours.

The cops were hot on my trail. Suddenly I came to a quick stop, that's when I bailed.

Into the woods I ran, with only the clothes on my back, and a forty-five in my hand.

Taking refuge among the trees, hiding among the hills, trying to avoided getting killed. Searching for a place to survive, beneath the dark sky.
My body was saturated with sweat, through the woods I ran for my life, like a hunted cat.

Hiding out in the night. Wishing upon the moon not to shine bright, and the stars to hold back the light.

Asking the wilderness not to give me up. I was sick and tired, left without fight. trembling in the night.

My eyes could see the police cars speeding by. With red lights flashing, down the open road they were sailing. From the dark woods I could hear the black crows wailing.

I had evaded the cops. Went into hiding, they kept on driving. Down an endless road, by night they drove.

Time rolled on. I was living quietly, given
a place to hide, with my gal by my side.
Listening to the satellite radio, waiting for
the word go.

Then I received a call, my blood begin
to boil, time spent with my woman had
come to an end. My mind begin to flow
again. I was like an eager, ready to take to
the wind.

Grand Theft Auto, putting on a show.
Leaving miles behind, like lightning
cutting into the passing of time.

I could feel a burning obsession rumbling
deep in my soul, Urging me to hit the
road.

Anxious to get behind the wheel, craving
the taste of a thrill.

Like a solder's thrill of victory. When he
conquers the enemy territory, immersed
in glory.
The sun had sunk into the night, making
plans with the pale moonlight.

I begin prowling the night, searching for a
fancy automobile. Lurking like a hungry
tiger ready for a kill.

I work along, living in a danger zone.
I located a car dealership, where the
cars were on display. I let myself inside,
without delay.

My heart was pounding, sick with
excitement, as I made my way. Grand
Theft Auto, is the only game to play.

I slipped into a fancy car, that shined like
a star. Down the freeway I went, riding
free and fast again, like wings upon the
wind.

With nerves of steel. At anytime I could
have be killed, living for a thrill.

I have respect for the rule of law, but I live
on the other side, this is how my lifestyle
has survived.

I realize, that there are repercussions for
my actions. To dream and then to die. My
brain is hyperactive most of the time, with
only danger stirring in my mind.

Flying down the freeway in a flow.
Undecided on which way to go. Into
a pass where the mountain rise, I had
no time for pause, looking for the right
turnoff. Beneath the open sky.

I would take the next turn, letting my fast
car run. Perhaps scarcely getting through,
flanked by the cops, flashing lights of red
over blue.

I was in a class of my own, a class where
no man belong. Living in distress, trying
to figure out which way was best.

Speeding through the towering mountains, to places my eyes had never beamed. Into the mighty valleys, rolling in a fast machine.

Ripping the roadways, hugging corners at high speed. Making my vehicle bob and weave.

I try to make sense of it all, like the twilights that rises and fall.

Living on the cutting edge, butterflies in my head. A sudden hush, I could feel the rush.

I like rolling in fast cars, I crave the danger that's involved, but soon I will be living behind high walls, and steel bars.

I live for the thrill. Not afraid to die, not afraid to kill. The cops were dead on my trail, they were closing in. I was flying down the freeway cutting through the wind.

Grand Theft Auto, with the engine humming like an echo, the end of the road was beginning to show. Desperation was in my face, the cops had invaded my space.

My journey would be coming to an end soon, I will be singing another tune, beneath the eyes of the moon.

Feeling the thrill, soon my blood would be spilled. I am a wanted man, from the cops I have ran.

Tearing through the streets, racing in
the black night, fleeing from the flashing
lights. Burning my high beams, cops were
on the scene.

They chased me long and hard, in their
black and white cars, racing beneath the
falling stars.

In hot pursuit, a shot in the dark, a flash
from the barrel of a gun.

I could feel the sting of a hot bullet,
tearing into my flesh, slowing my run. I
was in excruciating pain, moving in the
fast lane.

I started to bleed. Blood was gushing
from my side. Distracted by the lights that
blinded my eyes.
Speeding in the winds of time, trying to
escape the wrath of my crime.

The rays from the moonlight were filtering
through the trees, I continued to bleed,
feeling no ease.

Engaging in criminal behavior was my
only sin, but soon my soul could be
blowing in the wind.

Fire and smoke, blazes from my exhaust
pipes. My mind caught up in all the hype.
Led astray, accepting stolen money for
pay.

Down the crowded streets I sped. The
cops brought lots of heat, lucky I'm not
dead.

I bailed from my vehicle, running through a fields, overrun by tall grass and weeds, using my track and field speed.

I was in pain. The cops give chase, they begin to gain. I had been shot, losing blood fast, I didn't think I was going to last.

They unleashed the K9's. I could see them coming, moving at high speed, cutting into my lead.

Over a wooden fence I went. Fell into the backyard of a neighborhood, scrambling as fast as I could.

Running in the wind, my head was in a spin. grabbed by the cops, before I got away. the K9's had me pinned, they began to make me pay.

"Get down, get down on the ground," the cops shouted. "Don't move, hands behind your back."
They slammed me hard onto the street, knocking me off my feet.

I was stretched across the pavement. My body was drenched in sweat and blood. The bark of the K9's could be heard. This time I was the one to lose, my body was battled and bruised.

My job was boosting cars, now I'm living behind prison bars. Lost in the four winds, paying for my sins.

All my hopes and dreams have collided head-on with reality. My quest to win, has come to an end.

No one knew my name, just a man without a face, gone without a trace. If I die, no one will shed a tear, no one will cry.

drifting in a world of sin. Doing time, for my crime. Reminiscing of places I have been. Never realizing where the events of fate would have me go, locked behind prison walls, wasting away in a black hole down below.

"Grand Theft Auto"

AGENT EYES

Agent Eyes, flying high, getting
attention from all the guys. Living her
life as a secret spy.

An agent of the CIA, no one dare to
get in her way. Rooting out men, and
women of evil traits, handing them the
justice, that the law dictates.

Graduated from law school, being
familiar with all the rules. Knowing the
tricks of the trade, in the world of her
secret spy days.

Agent Eyes, 05. Dressed to kill,
penetrating the enemy strongholds,
harboring no fear, at the top of her skill.

Leading a secret life. Working
undercover for the CIA, she's a
government sacrifice, but not a wife.

Roaming through the world of
espionage, taking a deadly chance.
Trying not to show her wining hand.

All the guys say she's hot, skillful in
martial art, known for her point blink
shots. Blasting an automatic machine
gun, sending men for a run.

Prowling unfamiliar places, sought after
men she chases. They come to realized
that she is amazing, when she comes in
blazing.

Agent Eyes, CIA spy, jetting across the sky. Dispatched to hostile sites. Finding ways to get inside, during the heat of night.

Infiltrating enemy territory, busting up the illegal activity that brings them glory.

Managing to stay alive, in a world where it is hard to survive. Springing into action on code red, trading gunfire. Soon someone lays dead.

Agent Eyes, playing a game on the wild side, sporting a pair of dark shades, A common practice in her trade.

A scarf wrapped around her hair, maintaining a low profile, no time for flair.

Pretending to be shy, wearing a light smile. Fighting the faces of evil, men have tries to deceit her.

Making the big busts, once backup failed to arrive, her safety was deprived. Putting her in disgusted, no one does she trust.

She is not just talk. Carrying out a surveillance, in a midnight stalk. Gazing upon the enemy with the eyes of a hawk.

Protecting the nation, engaging in covert operations.

Forging through the hours, fighting
against men loaded with money and
power. She is not a little girl, simply
living in a big world.

Diverting assassination attempts.
Mounting break- ins, and wiretaps.
Alert, and on point with intelligent
work, even when she's hurt. She's CIA,
nothing gets in her way.

Being discreet, avoiding deceit. Careful
not to sit in the wrong seat. There are
those who would like to wipe her out,
enemies within, and enemies without.

She possesses animal like instincts, like
the wild tiger, walking with a swagger.

Packing a red hot forty-five, staying
alive, in a shootout she won't be the
one to die. Others would fall, bullets
ricocheting of the walls.

Her name is Lisa Ray, agent of the CIA.
From her agent eyes, men would run
and hide. Fighting crime aboard planes,
and high speed trains.

Wearing a tiny camera inside her
necklace of gold, gathering vital
information from whence the wind
blows.

Matching diamond earrings she carry
along, mounted with a very sensitive
microphone. Traveling the world, with a
rich taste for diamonds and pearls.

At times she dresses up in clothes of a disguise, wearing a hat that fades over her eyes. A long link coat, and pinstripe pants, activating a well thought out plan, out to get her man.

Once she refused to cry. taking out double spies, who worked both sides. She's deep cover CIA, in a quest to make the enemy pay.

When the time was right she went home, but never stayed too long. In the battlegrounds of the world she is destined to roam.

Across the world in a private jet, combating terrorism with allies she had never met.

Dispelling all neglect, dismissing all outdated operations, going high tech.

Playing a leading roll, to get in close, with the men who have gone rogue. Gathering secret intelligence, to take control.

Dialing up helicopter strikes, using the latest in military might. Blasting enemy sites, blazing up the nights.

"Oh, Agent Eyes, can I be your guy? Pretty CIA, give an ear to what I say."

"Fighting crime, come spend a little time. Oh, Agent Eyes of mine, I am mesmerized."

"In the face of danger when time was trying, into my eyes, you were a ray of sunshine."

"Never becoming a bride. Breaking my heart, holding hands with another guy. I will still love you, till the day I die."

"You wept for the one who left you along, whether right, or whether wrong, he drained the love right out of your heart, from him you drifted apart."

Here and abroad she makes her home, spending time along. Reliving the memories of her spy days,
Memories that seems to light up her face.

Reminiscing about what it would be like, had she chosen a different pass, would love have last?

Engaged in the fighting of crime, behind enemy lines. Explosions, and shootouts, never realizing what true love was all about.

Her life goes through uncertain phases. Often confusing, as a book with missing pages.

She lived a dangerous, and exciting life. An excellent job she would do, but her dreams would never come true.

Walking through the garden of scattered flowers, standing beneath the rain showers.

Faded marriage proposals, taken by the
winds, as the window of love closes. She
is left wandering through a bed of dying
roses.

Agent Eyes, 05, has lost the sparkle
that light up her smile. For her my soul
suffers, my heart pains, our lives took
a drastic change, nothing remains the
same.

Upon her pillow she cries, her tears
flows like rain. Once a lone spy, a
shining star to my eyes. She will be
concealing her love in a secret weapon,
till the day she dies.

"Sweet Agent Eyes"

SEASON LOVE CALLS

Hear the season love calls,
through the winter and
in the fall.

Hear it in the summer nights,
when the stars are
bright, someone
holding you
tight.

In the spring breeze,
among the birds
and bees.

The autumn colors of
fading green trees.
The red and
yellowing
leaves.

The springtime fragrant
that fills the air,
bringing lovers
together in
wonderful
pairs.

Season love calls,
when love is in
full bloom.

Blossoms of summer
flowers, upon
the face of
June.

The winter view, on
the seashore of
the ocean
blue.

Wild geese crossing
the night. Casting
silhouettes upon
the moon.

Saturating the lakes
on a spring
afternoon.

Hear the season love calls,
when the butterflies plays
amid the summer
bright green
grass.

Where the wild flowers
blossom, before
the season
pass.

Season love calls, in
the winter mountain
streams. In a
summertime
dream.

A snowy evening of
winter white, that
sparkles from
the stars of
night.

The freshly grown flowers,
brings a beautiful
scene, across
the winter
green.

Walking hand-and-hand,
falling in love.
Strolling the
summer
sands.

The pale winter sunrise.
Climbing the cold
mountain high,
to reach the
crystal
sky.

In the shades of fall, hear the
"Season Love Calls."

THE SLAMMER

The "Slammer," a prison hell hole,
where blood runs cold.

Where men live like animals behind
high walls, and steel gates. Thrust into
the jungle of their fate.

Locked in chains, like the wild and
the untamed. No one remembers their
names.

When I was very young, I had a fire
burning deep down in my belly. Pulling
at my soul, to play the tough guy roll.

Like the moon pulls at the tides of the
sea. A tough man I wanted to be.

I fell in with the wrong crowd. Men that
were living raw, above the law.

Got involved in hard crime. Didn't
recognize the warning signs. I was just a
child, with an undeveloped mind.

My parent tried to straighten me out.
Took away my free time; made me join
the boy scouts.

I thought they were wrong, before long,
I ran away from home.

The wind was in my face. The world was
my stage. Being young, like a new song,
I wanted to be seen, wanted to be heard.
Living in a fantasy world.

Running wild in the street. Thinking the world was at my feet, that life was candy sweet.

I got involved in an arm robbery, a man died. I was not the shooter, but had to take the long prison ride.

Execution was mandatory. I took a deal to spill the whole story.

Manslaughter was on the table, for a lesser charge, the DA say he was doing me a favor. I took the plea, now I'm during hard time on cellblock-D.

Behind fading concrete walls for the rest of my days, staring death right smack in the face.

I never thought this would happen to me. That this would come to be, living in misery.

An open cell, a walk into hell. Fighting to survive, till the day I die.

Stuck inside the stomach of the fire eating dragon, it is now my home. Put here by men who say this is where I belong.

They say I'm a killer, threw me in the Slammer, sending me up the river.

Life has dealt me a dead man's hand. From a shallow grave, in no man's land.

I was a hothead. Running with men committing violent crime, this is where I was led.

Where men live raw, but for me, it was a hard luck draw.

I have no love in my life, I never married a wife. In the love game I found no time to take part. Too busy doing the wrong things trying to be hard.

I'm Just beginning to face the facts, I have nothing, only the numbers stamped on my back.

The Slammer, the holding place for thieves, murders, and scammers.

Scheming to take whatever you got. The guards don't give a care, only waiting to take you out with a single shot.

This is one of the oldest prison that exist. The walls are thick, surrounded by a barbwire fence.

The cooling system rarely works. The big fan is broken, and never get fixed.

It gets awful hot in here during the summer, a cool breeze is impossible to find.

Sweat runs down your body like the sun has been magnified a thousand times.

There are no beautiful portraits that hangs on the walls, no paintings at all.

No pictures hang, no trees, or flowers
where the hummingbird sing.

The walls are bare and fading. The floors
seem to be decaying. No lovely view,
nothing sensible to do.

Just staring at the walls that I'm stuck
behind, doing hard time.

In the winter it gets cold as ice, I have
been frozen within an inch of my life.

The winter snow comes in, carried by
the hard wind. The heaters gets frozen. I
only regret the life that I have chosen.

There are no dreams to be realized here.
Early to bed, and early to rise, only the
dream to stay alive, another day before
you die.

The warden won't give me a break. He
shaved my head, cutting off my hair.

Threw me into the black hole, infested
with mice and rats. Did me cold,
stripped off my clothes.

I was on good behavior, he was doing
someone else a favor.

Nothing inside the Slammer is fair, set
up to take your morale.

I have begun to talk to myself, as if I
was someone else. Locked down in the
black hole for so long, my mind may be
gone.

It has been many days, since the sun
shined upon my face.

Barred from all human contact, no one
to watch my back. In the Slammer,
at anytime you are in danger of being
attacked.

Buried alive, deep in the walls of hell.
My tomb is the black hole, and the
inside of my cell. Pages of long hard
years, are draped over my coffin, my fate
has been sealed.

My body is soar, from sleeping on the
concrete floor.

Once and awhile, if I'm lucky. I get a
hard bed, to lay my aching head.

There is no feeling of being alive. Only
hidden tears, for my tough man eyes.

The cons in here are mean and cold.
Especially the ones that are serving life
without parole.

Cons with the capacity for deadly
violent. The ones whose families have
forgotten that they are alive; don't care
if they live, or die. Those that are curst,
inside this hell on earth.

Chaos is rampant throughout the whole
yard. There are fights here everyday.
Cons comes out swinging, hitting hard,
no one dare to pull them apart.

Men live like savages in this hell hole.
There are men let out of their cells,
only when they are locked in leg irons
and chains, they have nothing to gain.
Cold bloody killers, with muzzles on
their faces. Walking the grounds, barely
moving around.

Men have been brutally beaten until
they bled, left stretched across the
prison yard, later to be found dead.

Inmates on death row, pace the hard
concrete floor night and day. Wishing
and hoping that the executioner does
not show.

I have seen men walking around never
lifting their heads. Men that have
become the walking dead.

From the gates of their cell, wandering
through the prison of hell.

Their minds have been blown, their
memories have gone.

Shallow graves awaits them in the prison
cemetery, where some of the toughest
cons are buried.

My youth has faded. Wrestling with
the years trying to win an appeal. The
wrinkles in my face, has advanced to a
permanent stage.

It gets ugly in here, nothing pretty
about it. Men losing their lives, strong
men breaks down and cry.

Others pumping iron, always out of
line, ready to bust you up, for a dime.

There is nothing I can do. There must
be a way out of here, but I don't have a
clue.

All along, no where to roam. Soon
death will be my home.

"The Slammer"

I'M THE ONE TO BLAME

I'm the one to blame, I left you
crying in the rain. In a
heart of pain.

I'm so ashamed, my heart was
acting kind of strange,
when the rain came.

I should have known better,
I was afraid that there
was another fellow.

I'm the one to blame, when I
wandered away, searching for
the right words to say.

In misery I will spend my
time, paying for my
moral crime.

Wishing upon the stars
of blue, to make my
dream come true.

The dream of love
I have for you.

I'm the one to blame, so simple,
and so plain. Leaving you
crying in the rain.

I was caught up in the hands
of time, nothing good
was on my mind.
Drifting into another world,
a sneaky suspicion
started to swirl.

My eyes fail to see, the love
you had for me. obscured
by the blindfold of jealousy.

True love of burning flames
washed away by the
pouring rain.

Vanished in the winds.
not to be seen again.

Crying in the rain.
In a heart of pain.

"I'm The One To Blame"

THE CONCUBINE

Long before medieval time, Concubines
have lived vicarious lives, women who
became mistress, or secondary wives.

Cohabiting with a man although not
married, a wedding ring on her finger,
she would never carry.

One early morning I received a
telephone call from my boss. He asked
me to do him a favor, that would be a
lifesaver.

He instructed me to pickup his mistress
from the county jail. Put her on a train,
and send her back to whence she came.

I agreed to his request. When I was
about to leave, I told him I would do
my very best. He was pleased.

I arrived on time, with money in my
pocket to pay her fine.

Soon the gates open. Out of lockdown
she came, free from her shackles and
chains.

She wore black and white strips. Out of
the darkness she emerged into the light.

I could see the delightfulness on her
face, as she strolled out of the place.
glowing with glee, happy as can be.

At first glance, I was sent into a trance. Mesmerized, she was a portrait to my eyes. A new face, into my days. Released from lockdown. Her hands and feet were recently bounded.

She was attractive and young. My heart begin to sing a new song.

My life could have been in danger, she was a total stranger.

As we drove away I notice as she was staring back at the high prison walls. She seemed to be appalled.

She asked me for my name, I asked her the same.

Then she started to explain. She was a concubine, had been involved in petty crime.

Did time in the county jail, for a man who used her for illegal sales.

We made a stop, she wanted to change her clothes, somewhere along the winding road.

She had rosy cheeks. The clothes she changed into were very sleek.

The Concubine, one of a kind, I could tell. A woman as such my eyes had never beheld.

She displayed a sense of style and humor. We laughed and talked, went for a walk.

Eventually I told her that I would have to say good-bye. My boss advised me to put her on a train, and send her back to whence she came.

She begin to cry, that's when I wiped the tears from her eyes.

She moved in close, soon we were setting side-by-side into a lonesome ride.

She asked if she could stay with me, and be my concubine. That blew my mind.

I told her that would be nice, but I rather she be my wife.

Her beauty was as an ocean sunset. A woman I would have never met. Except my boss, had made the call.

I begin to envision a beautiful romance with a concubine, at some point in time.

My love for her begin to sprout like a young flower, after a summer rain shower.

She meant more to me than the price of silver and gold. For her hand in marriage I gracefully proposed.

This moment in time, perhaps it was
meant to be. My heart was over flowing
with excitement, and so much mystery.

A crazy part of me went cold. I could
feel the flames that burned wildly inside
her soul.

The spirit of fire that dominated her
desires, and refined her way of life that
someone else had chose.

I did not realize that my eyes were
blind to a lost soul, a personality phase,
expressed out of the medieval days.

We made a quick stop in front of her
place, to get makeup for her face .

She returned bearing perfume, spices,
and silk. I thought about giving her the
slip, speeding down the freeway letting
my car rip.

I refused to do such a thing, I had fallen
for a concubine, expressing traits from
medieval time.

She was wearing a lovely smile, then my
world seemed to be all blue skies.

Her glowing eyes, lit up the seaside.
Dazzled by her charm, my day was still
and calm.

I was starving for affection, love that
would fly in the right direction.

As time wore on, she became my wife. Wedding bells began to ring. Celestial choirs started to sing.

She mentioned that she did not envision ever getting married, no way could she tell. It must be a dream from a wishing well, to hear such beautiful wedding bells.

Married to a concubine, all odds were defied, but I had been taken for a ride.

She never bore children, or even one child. Often her heart would get sad, tears would roll down her eyes.

She was an artist. Setting for long periods at a time. Creating beautiful designs.

sketching figures day-after-day, never receiving pay.

Portraits of the mountain highs, kissing the skies, pictures of famous faces wearing smiles, colorful sad crowns that could make you cry.

sketches of men and women blasting the trails, she refused to put the drawings up for sail.

Excellent pictures she drew, but the decent way of life she never knew.

To please her I would speak of her beauty, and charm. Came bearing gifts, holding her in my arms.

She love expensive things, beautiful
clothes, and diamond rings. Faraway
trips, and vintage wine to sip.

Soon my money would disappears,
dining out at fabulous restaurants,
eating the most expensive meals.

I begin to realize that in this type of
marriage I didn't belong. Everything
started to turnout wrong.

When we went out on the town she
would get me into trouble, I would soon
discover.

She wasn't really trying, only being a
concubine.

Dancing wildly with all the men, at
times I wanted to get into my car, and
just ride, without a farewell, or a good-
bye.

I found myself fighting for her honor,
and at the same time I was trying to stay
alive.

Often I would awake at midnight,
she would be gone. I was living in an
unhappy home, left all along.

My boss fired me from my job,
contending that I had been busted.
Getting married to his mistress, never to
be trusted.

A Concubine, as living in medieval days, put me through hard times, in so many ways.

She didn't know how to be a decent wife, or live a normal life. No matter how hard we tried.

Going out at night, getting me into fights. I was charged with assault, trouble is all she brought.

Shoplifting, for designer clothes, back to the county jail she seemed to be drifting.

Taking high fashion shoes, as if she had nothing to loose. Using me like a fool.

I tried to change her ways, turn her into a desirable wife. As time went by I could see no improvement, not even a trace.

We got into a fight, she pull a long knife. She cut me up pretty good, blood was streaming down my arm, I was alarmed. Having her for a wife, was never sugar and spice.

The embrace of her arms were gentle, the kisses upon her ruby lips were soft and tender.

Our wedding vows she failed to remember. I took the recourse, and filed for a divorce.

She was conditioned only to be a
Concubine, a thing that was rooted in
her character till the end of time.

As time moved along, I put her on a
train, sent her back to whence she came.

I should have listen to my boss, so much
time has been lost.

I could see the tears in her eyes, as I
weaved good-bye. She was gone, but I
felt so all along.

Its insane, the way these things make
you feel. Since she came into my life
nothing was ever the same. From there
it was downhill, the time I spent with
her seemed to be so unreal.

Driven out of my mind, no time to
unwind. Lady barbaric, the burdens she
came bearing, are the burdens I had to
carry. I was to quick to marry.

I was betrayed by her beauty. Her
innocent smile, and the tears that fell
from her eyes.

I have started to piece my life back
together. The raging storm I have
weathered.

Hail to the Concubine, once a love of
mine, lost in the shadows of medieval
times. A woman whom life had defined.

"The Concubine"

OUTLAWS ON THE HIGH SEA

The sea was quiet and still, the sky was calm. My future was uncertain, this my heart could feel.

We were prowling the deep sea in the dead of night, beneath the oily black clouds that obscured the moonlight. We traveled aboard a ship call the "Dungeon,"

We moved in silence like a ghost. In search of a vessel that had been spotted in the waters near the Arabian seacoast.

It was carrying freshly printed thousand dollar bills, stolen from the federal reserve by men of magician skills.

Our mission was to seize the currency by any means necessary.

Even though it seemed to be a simple operation men would be killed, retrieving thousand dollar bills.

I worked for the world union sea patrol. Our unit was created to keep peace on the high sea, and fight piracy. To uphold the law, but instead we were living raw. Out laws on the run, under the gun.

Out laws on the High Sea. Where murderous and thieves would sometime flee. Vessels transporting illegal weapons and human cargo. Where hot merchandise and stolen money flow.

We spotted a huge boat up ahead. From a distance we followed as we were led.

We lowered our two jet boats into the water.

With a burst of speed we closed in fast, like a hungry lion running down it's prey, cutting through a precise pass.
Wearing rubble face mask, and scuba gear. Out laws with no
sense of fear. Giving no thought to who will die, or who will be killed.

We were heavily armed with bazookas and machine guns, in a hurry to carry out this assignment before the rising sun.

With the loudness of a bullhorn we sent out commands. "you on deck, hear this," said the captain.

"We are ready to blow a hole right through your boat. Tonight you will be sleeping with the sharks, or you will be doing a dead man's float."

"We came for the money you are carrying on board your vessel, the "Calimaroo." Obey our orders is what you must do."

"No one will get hurt if you do what I say. We will let you go, and tomorrow will be a good day."

"throw the money overboard, is all you have to do. Then you can be on your way."

Suddenly shots rang out. Hails of bullets began raining down on our vessel like a swarm of bees. We took cover and let go a round from our bazooka. Boom!

The Calimaroo exploded into flames, shooting high to the sky. Men were hurled into the sea. Fire and smoke burned in the night, looming above the battle site.

The huge boat was going down. Men from our vessel hit the cold water dressed in their scuba gear, but there was no money to be found.

One of our men suddenly spotted an airtight container that had surfaced. We brought it aboard, bingo! Thousand dollar bills filled the inside, a treasure before our eyes.
We climbed back into our vessel and sped away, men who try to stop us would have to pay.

We were on a roll, taking control. In search of money, diamonds and gold.

We traveled swiftly across the dark waters, I knew our days were numbered. A dream came to me in a midnight slumber.

We carried out illegal schemes day in, and day out. Trying to put our hands on as much money as possible in defiant of the law. This is what we had become, this is what we were all about.

Commandeering expensive vessels when the occupants were just out boating, leaving men in the water floating.

We were dangerous and bold. Outlaws working the sea patrol. On an illegal roll, masterminds in crime.

Once bona fide as the world union sea patrol, performing our duties, just doing what we were told.

Somewhere down the line we took a wrong turn, for human life we had no concern.

Living in a fools paradise. Romancing strange women, but never taking time for a wife.

We traveled the North Atlantic to the South Pacific, making our way across the untamed waters like an invisible ghost, passing through the African Coast. By day staying out of site, roaming the waters by night.

Plowing the Indian Ocean, setting things in motion. Hijacking marked ships, in the course of their trips.

Through the Arabian sea we traveled the waters through, terrorizing across the ocean blue.

When I was very young I started running with some of my next of kin. They were sentenced to fifteen years in the pen, but the life of crime had gotten under my skin.

I was living in vain, nothing good had I became. Left with deep scars on my body and in my brain. I can still feel the pain.

A while back we were disbarred from the ranks of the world union sea patrol. The black market had us under their control, we had been bought and sold.

We strayed along, never returning home. Hanging on to the tail of the wind, wearing sea patrol uniforms time and time again. We used them at will, stopping sea traffic and making all kind of illegal deals.

We were wanted men, our faces were against the wind. Placed on wanted posts across the nation, in places we had never been.

Intruding on protected site, racing in the night beneath the pale moonlight.

Hiding in shadowy places, wearing disguises on our faces, seeking out easy prey, at the fall of darkness, or in the light of day. Masterminds, in the sea of crime, raiding and misbehaving.

Out Laws on the High Sea, is not what I wanted to be.
The old devil himself must have chose this life for me.

I turned a blind eye to the law, learning from the bad practices my eyes had saw.

Prone to survive, with an underworld tide. We were men of desperate means, in search of empty dreams.

As time sailed on. Out of the dawn came the rising sun. the day was rather fair, my eyes got lost in the sun glare.

The men were exhausted, the rugged sea had took it's toll. We needed food and rest before we journey any farther, then later we would pickup and go.

We cast anchor in the waters near a secluded island, where the native people presented us with colorful beads, as we rested beneath the shade of the palm trees.

Bees were buzzing in a rising mist, birds were composing their tunes on a tropical afternoon.

The natives served coconut milk and roasted pig.
We were drinking wine and having a good old time.
Dancing, running in the sands, embracing romance.

To us it was a fabulous island retreat, the native language we did not speak, but for things of value such as money, gold, or diamonds we continued to seek.

Out laws on the run, having a little fun. Here we were not recognized by anyone.

As the day wore on the sunset was fading into the twilight, in the face of night. Above the sky, the moon begin rising high.

Some of the men were having second thoughts about returning to our mother ship, the "Dungeon."

They had a suspicion that some mysterious event would take place before daybreak, so we stayed awake, watching the night, hoping everything would turnout right.

Suddenly a shot rang out. It was a signal sent by one of our men to get our attention.

He had discovered a pure gold statue that stood in the midst of the resting place for the dead, this is where we were led.

Drunken with wine, and intoxicated with women, we threw a rope around the golden statue, dragging it out to the seashore.

In an instant men came storming toward us shooting semiautomatic rifles.

A night of fun we had blew. These men were pirates, they were after the gold statue too.

One of our men went down. We quickly scattered about and hit the ground, returning fire, unleashing lots of gun rounds.

It turned into an out law warfare, raging in the night. Men laid dead, caught between an out law fight.

We fought our way back to the mother ship. Leaving the golden statue behind, too many men were dying.

The crane that was affixed to our ship reached down and pulled our boats from the water, bringing them back aboard the Dungeon.

We traveled the sea months at a time, leaving the states behind. The sea was our home, a danger zone. A water jungle in which we roamed.

Aboard the Dungeon we carried inflatable rafts, and two of the fastest jet boats in the world.

We needed speed, to jet across the rough waters with ease, and the quietness of the inflatable rafts for silence. To take flight, or engage in unforeseen fights, like ghosts in the night.

Out Laws on the High Sea, living mean and living raw, living on the wrong side of the law.

A misguided mindset, you can bet. Ask us about love, we don't know nothing about that.

The day had come and gone. We were on the look out for vessels that traveled the waters along.

The sun was resting at the edge of the sea, just waiting around, for sundown.

We lowered the two jet boats into the water. We begin moving through the waves with quietness and ease, but like sharks we were moving with speed.

Our eyes were surprised to see, a family of huge whales, swimming in the depths of the crystal blue sea, traveling wild and free.

They made a splashing sound, with their gigantic tails rising up from the waters then going back down.

In the vicinity of our vessels they came very close, spurting water from their blowholes.

With her massive tail, one of the whales raised up from the waters, capsizing one of the jet boats thrusting us into the sea.

We cried out for help, then pulled from the waters by other crew members who heard our plea. The overturned boat, resurfaced and began to float.

The massive whales were headed for the city that looms beneath the sea of crime, drifting with the tides of time.

Where old pirates ships have been swallowed up, and where volcanoes had once erupt.

The ends of the sunrays was filtering through the distant sky, disappearing from our eyes. The light of the moon would be coming into view soon.

We turned our attention to a huge fishing boat. Tracked it down, threaten to blow the crew out of the water using grenades, and machine gun rounds. They surrendered to us, just after dusk.

We went aboard the big rusty vessel. The crew pretended to be only fisherman's, but we knew they were diamond traders, and sea raiders.

The top deck was overrun with all kinds of fish. Some had been gutted, sliced, and put on ice.

But inside the fish sparkled the ice of diamonds. We took the diamonds, and left the fish behind, running out of time.

Not so long ago, when I was too young to know. We were notorious for hard street crime. Lost out of our minds, living on the edge of time, that had unwind.

Barely sleeping, one eye open, and the other eye peeping. We were on a roll, taking armor trucks for silver and gold.

Living hard, taking diamonds that were under guard. Robbing banks using armor tanks.

The sea had adopted us, this is what we knew, in the light of view. Out laws on the run, vilified and put under the gun. Moving throughout the seacoast, like a ghost.

Time was moving on, winter was closing in. The weather condition was terrible and the sky was pale. We looked for a safe passage across the water trail.

Up ahead black clouds were draping across the sea. As if they beckoned for us to come near into a gateway, that leads to hell. Darkness had consumed the day.

The sky threaten to bring rain. Then the rain came. It began to fall, jumping on the waters hard and heavy like the sound of frogs.

The Dungeon moved swiftly through the rain, grinding forward through the rumbling sea that swirled untamed.

In this segment of the sea the water boiled as if in a huge pot, with flames beneath it that were very hot.

Rising steam acted like fog, reducing our visibility forming a big blob. We could hear the cry of the sea creatures as they bellowed out their night calls.

We were driven into the teeth of the sea, that had chewed up old ships and spit them out. Carried by the curses of the winds. Here men had met their doom, the sea is now their resting place, and the sky is their tomb.

Tonight one of us is marked to die. To be tossed outside of time, never to return again. Our eyes were upon the waters that held the sign.

In the distant waters we could see a flashing light, flickering in the night. The Dungeon was the target of a strike, our crew dug in deep, prepared to fight back.

Suddenly a grenade hit the side of our ship, rocking the big vessel like a baby's cradle.

We tried to run, changing directions making a quick turn. Another incoming strike was sweeping through the waters, but we were gone. The sea was about to become a battle zone.

We lowered our two jet boat into the bubbling water. In order to succeed, we would use power and speed.

We came upon the adversary ship and begin attacking from both sides, swinging wide, blood was in our eyes.

I had never seen a ship like this before, it was like something out of the medieval days, plowing through the massive waves.

The huge black vessel was making it's way through the waters like a dinosaur. The strangest ship my eyes have ever saw.

Hot fire and flying lead, were coming from the strange ship piercing the waters where we tread.

We continued to move swiftly across the rogue sea, unleashing a powerful blast from the barrel of our bazooka. Boom!

Sounds of the loud explosion echoed across the waters. We let go another round. Boom! Fire and smoke took to the night, looming over the site.

The big strange ship was rocked on it's side. Some men die, others survived.

We moved in on the ship quickly. Some of our men searched the waters below, when ordered to do so.

We climbed aboard the strange vessel. Men laid dead, others were afraid. It was like a graveyard up there, with the look of death, and the smell of strong wine. Men were like zombies, they seemed to have been dead for a long time.

In exchange for their lives, the remaining men chose to tell us the where about of the money and gold.

We took everything they had, then headed back to the Dungeon as time passed.

We celebrated the find, drinking whiskey and wine, then left the big strange ship behind.

As time moved on we were chased by three gunboats. Men looking to collect the bounty that had been placed on our heads, whether we were brought in alive, or dragged in dead.

At the same time the coast guard blockaded our path in the waters that laid ahead. Near the mouth of the sea near a sand bed.

They moved in on us with grenades and machine guns. They came blasting from below, the Dungeon was about to blow.

Over the side of our ship we went. Diving into the deep blue sea, in an attempt to flee.

As I swam away I could see the Dungeon explode into fire and smoke. Big red flames raised to the sky, a few of our men had died.

I was pulled from the cold water by the coast guard. We hung around, just long enough to watch the tail of the Dungeon go down.

I was tried and convicted for my high sea crimes, now I'm doing a life of hard prison time.

My mind was not very sound, I guess you might say this is where I was bound.

Like a wild creature we rumbled the deep waters of the seven seas. Searching for easy ships to prey upon, like those that travel the waters along.

Invading protected spaces, wearing mask on our faces. Bursting on the scene, ambushing and bush wracking. Spotting lone ships then attacking.

Getting into shootouts, with other men who behaved exactly the same, powerful weapons we were never without. It was an out law game.
Men who have had their mind scarred, men who learned to play the game hard.

It doesn't matter whose wrong or whose right. In the underworld it's an out law fight.

Men trying to do their best, making their own laws like the wild, wild west.

Constantly looking over their shoulders, trying to figure out the smart thing to do, fleeing when no one pursue.

The sea was in my blood, and my blood is in the sea. I never can leave the past behind, living out my days on borrowed time. Like a ghost, that roamed the waters of the seacoasts.

Perhaps this is the way it was meant to be. Time has chose this life for me, living in the shadows of reality.

"Out Laws On The High Sea"

ANGEL OF LOVE

Oh, Angel of Love, come down from
the heavens, among the stars
above. Bearing the
cradle of love.

With soft wings, and a lovely voice
that sings. With heavenly eyes,
innocent as a child. Pure
as the ocean sky.

Awake me with thy gentle touch.
guide me with thy arms
of gold. Embracing
my soul.

Cover me with thy tender mercy.
filling my days, with joy
and gladness with
thy loving
ways.

Bring a smile to my face when I am
longing to cry. Turn on thy light
of love. Let it shine from
the heavens
above.

Angel of Love, pure as the driven snow.
keep me in the treasures of thy
hands, whether on high
or down below.

Let me fly with the wings of love,
and with the glory
of a dove.

Oh, Angel of Love, gentle in the
wind. Into my heart
grow thy love
within.

"Sweet Angel of Love"

THE VAGABOND

The "Vagabond," a fugitive on
the run. Moving swiftly through
the night. Destination, his
hometown. packing a stolen gun,
and he won't be looking for fun.

His soul is raging, for ways to
erase bitter memories, and broken
dreams of yesterdays, his heart
chases.

Breaking rules, living in his own
solitude. He knows the law, but
he's living raw.

He is coming to square things, for
a double cross. A man put hands
on his money, and took it all.

The man must pay the price, for
running off with his wife, and
ruining his life.

Having him sent to jail, on
charges for a store they both
robbed, leading to the dismissal
of his job.

He once was standing tall, but
his world went spiraling into a
downfall.

The Vagabond, carrying an
automatic forty- five. He doesn't
care whether he live, or die. The
man he use to call his friend may
not be left alive.

Wandering the days along, going
through life without a home.

Choosing the hard course of
survivor, since the day he was
born, whether right, or wrong.

The difficulties of his days would
be prolonged.

Getting lost in the crowded
streets, picking pockets, with
hands of deceit.

Committing violent crime,
blaming others for his hard times.

He shot the man, he once
called his friend. He came to
town looking for sweet revenge.
Running through the day, trying
to get away.

Walking in haste, giving no
time to waste. Just moving on,
whistling down the railroad
tracks.

Clinging to a sack, thrown across
his shoulder, carried on his back.

Hopping on a freight train, with
blood stains still on his hands. His
body is suffering from aches and
pains.

Leaving a violent trail, along the
endless rails. Sleeping in boxcars,
no medication to heal his scars.

Hitchhiking in the night,
avoiding the bright lights.
Changing his name, trying not to
look the same.

The Vagabond, a fugitive on the
run. Frostbitten and baked by the
sun.

Migrating like birds on the
feathers, in all kind of weather.

Rain, hail, anything to avoid time
in jail, giving up all rights to the
U.S. mail.

Doing whatever his mind deem to
be the best, to evade an arrest.

Through the eyes of the world he
is recognized as a drunken hobo,
with no decent place to go.

Constantly roaming the cities,
and towns, looking for a place to
bed down.

Committing arm robbery, putting
his hands to stealing. Hiding out
from a capture, in a vacant house
ceiling.

Beneath the overpass bridges, and the city limit ridges. There he makes his bed, barely suitable to lay his head. Whcrc no one wants to tread.

Don't come around, when he's on the prowl, or you may be gunned down.

He will only hightail it to the next town, and will not be sticking around.

Begging for money, beneath the cloudy skies, or when the day is sunny.

Waiting for the night, putting out the lights, drinking and gambling at underground cock fights

A holdup at a convenient store, unleashing trouble wherever he go.

No sense of keeping the law, or doing what is deem to be right, blazing up the trails at night.

The Vagabond, for life he has no concern, constantly on the run, packing a stolen gun.

His face wears deep frowns, Reflecting the long years, for which he has been around.

Blackballed, from getting a job in
his chosen field, or any position
that seem to be real.

Leaving no witnesses to his crime,
covering up the timelines. Using
mind over matter, living in his
own shadow.

A hobo, a little slumber on the
boxcar floor. Living on the low, he
has become a pro, evading the law
wherever he go.

To dream, and then to die. The
future is fading right before his
eyes.

He once lived in the house of
prosperity, and wisdom. Then it
came crashing down. Now he is
living a life that's unsound.

Dealing with the cost, of a mind
that is lost.

Gone is his unique ideas, and
the bridge he dreamed to build.
Connecting the technology field.

Sleeping with the rats, fighting off
the bats, in his world of hobos,
where anything goes.

Drunken most of the time.
Drowning in cheep wine, feeling
that life has left him behind, and
carried away his mind.

The power of his brain seem to fad, his eyes gazes upon a shadow grave.

Chain smoking cigarettes, hooked on all kind of booze. In possession of burglary tools.

Staggering for days, unsteady on his feet, with the sun full on his face.

Nothing in his world seem to change, as if frozen in time. Moving in slow motion with eyes of the blind.

It's not likely his life will last, due to the mountain of troubles he have had.

Longevity has it's place. His struggle with life has robbed him of full days.

His zest for life once burned like flames, that comes out of the mouth of dragons. Carried by the winds, nothing to remain, his trail may soon come to an end.

When the hard winds came, he was forced to make a change. Spending his time riding on a freight train.

Living out of a sack, going through life with old clothes on his back.

Riding on the rails, covering a violent trail. Constantly on the run, with nothing new under the sun.

"The Vagabond"

SINGING LOVE SONGS

Singing Love Songs, the whole day long.
Reminiscent of you,
since you been
gone.

Feeling the melody deep inside,
visions of your love
play about my
eyes.

Harmonizing with the night,
slow dancing with
the starlight.

Singing Love Songs just for you.
Waiting for your love,
that is long
overdue.

Colorful lyrics with a gentle tone.
making a request
to forgive my
wrongs.

Singing Love Songs, with a touch
of flair, taken from the
sun glare, when
love is in
the air.

Painting the skies blue, with love
songs that remind me
of you.

Love songs of harmony, with
words of clarity, for the
eyes of the heart
to see.

Love songs of faraway nights,
that have journeyed
beyond the stars
of bright.

Leaving behind the memories
for making love songs,
with a glow of
delight.

Singing Love Songs, that calm the
fear of forever losing you.
Love songs that the
heart can
feel.

Flowing with a gentle touch,
for a sensitive
appeal.

Love songs of springtime, words and
rhyme. Autumn leaves and summer
breeze. Spring flowers
and winter
showers.

Singing Love Songs, that resides in my
heart, and sleeps in my mind.
Taken from memories
frozen in
time.

With a unique style, that can
wipe the tears
from your
eyes.

Love songs that are yet unknown,
for you only, do they belong.
Sung with a mellow
tone.

"Singing Love Songs"

A THUG IN TOUCH WITH LOVE

I have been labeled a thug, but I'm
"In Touch with Love."

There is a myth that I find ways to rob
and steal. To get what I want, and do
what I will. This is not real, it is not a
thrill.

I fell in love with a beautiful woman
who bored my child, for her I almost
died. She was the diamond of my eye.

I treated her very nice, she was going
to be my wife. She took advantage
of my kindness, and exploited my
weakness. She used me in a deceitful
way, I must have been led astray.

I know it was wrong, but I was
dominated by love, persuaded to go
along.

I thought of my woman as pure, I love
the way she made me feel.

My only motive was to please her.
When she would cry, I took to
whatever means to make her smile.

Picked up a gun, went on a midnight
run. Bucking for easy money, to please
my honey.

The cops profiled me as a thug, but I
was In Touch with Love.

I don't do small jobs, or go around
jacking cars, and no one can tell you
whom I robbed.

I don't do drive-bys, I am most
civilized, except
when I am hypnotized, by the magic
of love, and for that I have apologized.

I know what goes on in the streets of
the city. In the high rises, among the
skylines, where men have no pity.

I don't stand on street corners. I live
my life fighting for my woman's
honor.

I am real, not the one to squeal. For
less, I have seen men killed.

Like a roaring lion, I only move
within my territory, looking for the
glory.

The only different is I have been
marked as the prey, but I refuse to be
captured like game. So here I stay.

I once was involved in an arm
robbery, for that I am sorry.

I became entangled in an awful mess.
trying to keep my woman happy, she
demanded the very best.

This was not the way love suppose to
be, I was too blind to see.

The cops accused me of being a thug,
but I was In Touch with Love.

I went to jail, then made bail. Back
to the streets again, going to the same
old places I had previously been.

Toting a gun, doing the same old
things I had already done.

Living in a bad neighborhood, I
would have taken wings, and flown
away only if I could.

I am not a Casanova, but I was trying
to get over. Love stole my heart, when
I was trying to play the part.

I begin to drink whiskey and wine.
Hanging out pretending to be having
a goodtime. Getting drunk, to the
bottom of the gutter I had sunk.

living in the land of the blind. I think
it must have blew my mind.

My woman was in love with high
fashion, for this she was obsessed.
New shoes, or a pretty dress, she
wanted no less. A shiny car, and
plenty of money to travel far.

I put my hands on enough money to
keep a smile on her face, footing the
bills, for her expensive taste.

We were riding high, scheming for
money, until a man had to die. Too
many secret tales, we tried to hide.

Caught of guard, when a jewelry store was robbed. I was busted, and disgusted.

Trying to carry out a plan, to put a diamond ring on my woman's hand.

Dealing with her I was none the wise, trying hard to keep a glow in her eyes.

Throwing caution to the wind, forgetting where I had come from, or where I have been.

Not remembering of what I am comprised, in the halls of poverty I use to reside.

I went on a crusade to escape the dungeon of doom, that had been thrust upon me like a plague, I was being consumed.

A burden of neglect, that had been hung around my neck.

I never meant for anyone to die, only to satisfy a burning desire, that reflected from my woman's eye.

I was caught up in the hype of being a high roller. Breaking the law; living raw.

The cops say I'm a thug, but I was In Touch with Love.

My woman gave me a thrill, that's
just the way she made me feel, on the
contrary she almost had me killed.

She begin to entertain other men,
asserting they were only friends.

Late one night I came home, she had
been left all along.

She started to cry, I could not
withstand the tears that fell from her
eyes.

A friend she said, had committed an
awful sin upon her bed. I was being
misled.

I packed my gun, going to get
something done. As I stepped out
side, a strange man was standing
nearby, He had the look of a tough
guy.

He was trying to take my life.
Without delay he moved in quickly,
and stabbed me with a knife.

I struggled to draw my gun, got off
two rounds hitting him twice. Bang!
Bang! Smoke from my nine millimeter
faded into the night.

Blood was gushing from my aching
body, The face of death was staring
straight into my eyes. hanging on to
life, I was barely alive.

I grabbed my side, clinching my
bleeding wound, squeezing it tight.
Trying to make it through the night.

He turned, when he tried to run,
staggered into the street. There he fell
hitting his head, there he laid dead.

I was losing blood fast, I didn't think
my life was going to last.

Bad vibes were racing through my
head, I collapsed, and there I bled.

I could hear the screaming sirens of
the police cruisers, and ambulance, as
they came to the rescue. I think it was
quite a few.

I was released from the hospital the
following day. My woman had packed
up, and gone away.

She walked out on me; took my child,
to never say good-bye. For her honor I
was willing to die.

Her love for me went blowing in the
wind. I never thought this love would
ever end. As time wore on, I was
sentence to do hard time in a nearby
state pen.

For the death of that stranger, I was
not to blame, I'm an innocent man.
Self-defense, is only common sense.

I tried to play the game well, trying
to stay above burning hell, but the
system had already numbered my
prison cell.

I guess it was meant to be, living a
life of misery.

I was misled, the woman played with
my head. I wish it had not been, her
love I tried to win.

I fell hard for her, like the stars that
falls from the sky above.

The cops called me a thug, but I was
In Touch with Love.

"A Thug In Touch With Love"

STOLEN KISSES

Stolen Kisses, is what I've been missing.
when we played
counting the
stars.

Walking in the shade,
strolling the
park.

Stolen Kisses, on a mild summer day.
Romantic games
we used to
play.

When we run through
the scattered sands,
making lovely
plans.

Singing in the winds, touched
by the sun. Stolen
kisses, for our
love to
burn.

The touch of your
Fingertips, a kiss
on your
lips.

A smile upon your
face, the look
in amaze.

Stolen Kisses, that melts my heart,
with memories,
never will I
discard.

Like precious diamonds that
never grows
old.

Sweet memories,
my heart will
always
hold.

The glitter of gold,
that rises in
time.

Sweet memories of Stolen Kisses.
playing with
my mind.

The poetry of our dreams, love
blossom beyond
extreme.

As if magic is in the sky,
reflecting the
love that's
in your
eyes.

A burst of starlight,
a kiss in the
night.

Lost in wonder,
and delight.

Laughter from the heart,
in a bliss
of fun.

Stolen Kisses, when
the day is
done.

Soft winds on the seashore,
making lovely
sounds.

Stolen Kisses, until
The sun goes
Down.

"Stolen Kisses, is what
I've been missing."

OUT OF THE TREETOP

Out of the treetop he came, looking for the rain. He was known as the "Big Tree," a huge sight, for the eyes to see.

He lived high up in the forest trees, living among the birds and the bees.

He built his home similar to a honeycomb, with features like a bird's net, making it the very best.

He covered it with large green leaves, taken from the surrounding trees. No one knew his name, some just called him the Tree Man. His way of life no one could understand.

He had no family members, no one to resemble. A friend to the wolves, and the bears. They, he would sometime feed, whenever there was a need. His body was somewhat covered with woolly hair.

Big Tree was very tall, standing seven feet four, bending over whenever he entered an open door.

He fashioned his boots out of rattlesnake skin, that wrapped around his legs, and held tightly with a wooden pen.

He woven his trousers out of gigantic leaves, that extended down to his knees.

Upon his head he wore a black polecat hat, with a white striped tail, extending past his neck, down to his back, to be exact.

During the cold winters, Big Tree dressed up in handmade alligator boots, bear skin, and rawhide, with a dagger hanging from his side.

Like the beast of the wild, he ate his food raw, with a strong jaw.

Living along, he devoured large chunks of meat right off the bone.

He often gave thanks to the rising sun. with hands held high, he spoke words to the sky.

After dark, he used old oil lamps, to give light to the camp. Lighting up the trees, that gave way to silhouettes upon the leaves.

He love the falling rain. When the hard rain came, the Tree Man would run beneath the showers, for maybe an hour. Spending time dancing in the pouring rain. Spinning around, listening to the sounds, across the plain.

Lifting his large hands high toward the sky. Singing a song that was heard for miles. A song that no one had ever heard, nor men, women, boys, or girls

He welcomed the rain to fall upon his face, playing with the wild animals, he gave chase.

Allowing the pouring rain to wash down his long shaggy beard. He love the way it made him feel.

On any given day, when the hard rain had made its way. You could see the Big Tree, dancing in the falling rain, happy, wild, and untamed.

He only came to town, when he thought no one was around. Mostly after dark, that's when the dogs begin to bark.

He only looked for food, to take from the garbage cans. If anyone came near, he often ran.

A report from the evening news. A woman had been abused. She was found dead, dragged from her bed.

It appeared that she had put up a hard fight, before she was carried away into the night.

The sheriff had found one of her shoes. Big Tree had been accused.

A search party was organized to hunt down the killer. Evidence was gathered from her room, and from the stains upon her pillow.

The search party went looking for a man, who had been seen running in the rain.

They clung to powerful guns, dogs and all searching the woods, for he, whom some called the Tree Man. He was said to be insane.

They hunted all through the day, and into the night. Carrying their guns, and their flashlights.

From that period forward, this day was remembered for the pouring rain, and the legend of the notorious Tree man.

The search party grew angry, and impatient. They soon transformed themselves into a blood thirsty mob. This heinous crime they were desperate to resolve.

Big Tree was spotted coming down from a huge oak tree. This was where he would rather be.

Gunshots were fired by the mob, for blood they were starved. Flashes of gunfire sent sparks flying through the darkness. No one was hit, it was a clear miss.

“Hold it right there Big Man. Don’t you move, or your life you will lose.” One of the men said.

Big Tree started to run, from the angry mob that were carrying the guns. in a quest to get away, to live another day.

He was moving fast, trying to hang on to the past, to make his life last. Running through the trails, when the wolves begin to wail.

The mob gave chase, making plans to put him in a cage. Again shots were fired, the men were winded and tired. Running after Tree Man, with powerful guns within their hands.

The ground was soaking wet. They surrounded the Big Man, trapping him with a net.

He let go a loud yell. As that of a wild beast, twisting and turning, trying to escape before his body fell.

The mob were stirring about, holding back thoughts to take him out. Trying to put his huge body down. Finally he fell to the rain soaked ground. Breathing hard, his clothes had been ripped apart.

A muzzle was strapped and fastened over his mouth. His hands, and feet were locked in heavy chains, no way could he get out. He was said to be wild and untamed.
Two shots were fired into the air. Bang! Bang! Warning others who were there, that a trap had been set, and Big Tree had been captured in a net.

The mob threw him in a cage, they were in raged. They slapped a padlock on the door, he could not run as he had done before.

The ravens flew in, filling the nearby trees. They knew the Tree Man well, watching as he fell. These birds he would often feed.

They would fly down close, to the winding road. Angrily engaging the men as they fluttered their wings and loudly crowed. In a sense, for the Tree Man's defense.

The mob hauled him back to town, in the back of a pickup truck. People came from miles around, to lay eyes on the notorious Tree Man, who was seen running in the rain. A woman was found dead. Big Tree had been accused, based upon what someone had said.

Blood was streaming down his face. The onlookers were pumped up in rage.

He was dragged out of the cage, and chained to a steel pole. Standing in the rain with only tree leaves, for clothes.

Fierce wind ripped into his shivering body with the winter cold. Tearing right through his soul.

The mob hurled rocks and stones at him. He had previously been hit on the head with a tree limb.

He was in despair, the town people just stood and stared.

The hard rain, once again came. He was dragged into court, attached to a ball and chain, that bound his feet and hands.

They threw him through the courtroom's door, rain water fell from his huge body, dripping onto the courtroom's floor.

Guilty as charged the judge read, for the assault perpetrated upon the woman who lay dead.

The courtroom erupted in cheer. The people called for him to be killed.

Suddenly, the Big Tree rose up. He cried out in a loud voice, "no, no, Let me go."

He overpowered one of the sheriffs, grabbed his gun, and begin to run. His chains broke, he had lost all hope.

He started blasting. Bang! Bang! Bang! Three shots rang out, people scattered about. The Big Tree, broke out of the ball and chains. Out of the courtroom he came. Bailing in the rain.

Back to his domain he fled, a place where no man dare to tread.

The mob went after him, armed and dangerous were all of them. Geared to shoot him down, and bring him back to town.

They kept their hands close to the pistols that were strapped to their sides, determined to bring him back dead or alive.

The mob was approaching the deep dark woods. Suddenly violent wolves exploded with powerful force, from beneath the weeds, crouching near the trees, standing atop tall rocks, the mob quickly stopped.

The wolf pack begin to growl, they were on the prowl. They were fierce, imposing their will.
With a swift leap they were upon the mob instantly, exposing their cutting edge teeth, and sharp fangs, cutting of the entrance lanes.

The mob finally got off several shots, the wolves bailed out. Avoiding deadly rounds, that would put them down. They would do anything at hand, to save the Tree Man.

Two grizzly bears reared up on their hind legs. Blocking the darkening road, whence the men drove. The mob would scatter and run, one of the vehicles was overturned.

The mob grabbed their guns and begin to blast, the grizzly bears could not last.

The Tree Man was spotted running and dancing in the rain. Without warning he was shot down like a mad dog. It was the sheriff who made the call.

So long to Big Tree, who was never given a chance, to live his life as a normal man.

Moment later, the real killer boarded a train, riding out of town through the pouring rain. He no one tried to stop, not even a cop. He was the guilty man, with gun in hand.

"Out of the Treetop"

BETRAYAL

Betrayal, by those who are
destined to fail, leaving
behind a dark trail.
Whistling in the winds,
pretending to be your
friend.

They came bearing wicked
deeds, never meaning to
please, in a scheme to
deceive. Trickery was up
their sleeve.

Masquerading as my friend,
but they were enemies
within.

Guns for hire, and
diamonds for sale. Based
upon the blind eyes of
betrayal. Criminal minds,
working overtime.

Hiding their faces, lurking
in the corner of dark places.

Gun shots in the night. A
deception comes to light. I
was doubled crossed, by the
hearts that are lost.

My money was taken, that's
when I was awaken. I put
up a hard fight, sent reeling
in the night.

Left along in the scorching
desert, beneath the cold
black sky. Left to die,
betrayal was the reason why.

My sense of trust has forever
changed, it will never be the
same.

Seduced by deceitful eyes.
they pretended to cry, it was
just foolish love in disguise.

I struggled to stay alive,
with no one by my side.

Backstabbed, betrayed with
a flair. When I was taught
to be fair. love has vanished
in thin air.

Betrayal, by the one's who
are taking sides, telling lies.
It doesn't matter whether I
live, or whether I die.

Clearing out my bank
account, ripping off the
whole amount.

They tried to made me
understand, that it was
good for my future plans,
like a walk in the sands.

Friends and foe alike. have
stabbed me in my back.

I continue to mount a fierce
fight, staying up late at
night.

Like a moment frozen in
time, peace I could not find.

They are dancing with the
devil, with hearts of stones
forever.

Hearts that hides from the
truth, is nothing new, but
old as the morning dew.

Betrayal, chasing an empty
dream, searching for shade
in the eye of the sun, when
there is none. Going far and
beyond the extreme.

They ravaged me with soft
words, my ears believed
what I'd heard.

I was lavished with
affection, hooked up with
the wrong connections.

They tried to take my
mind, but I found a way to
unwind, by staying in touch
with real time.

My drink was laced, with
a toxic trace. Without
remorse, or without
disgrace.

They walked in silence.
Spoke words that could not
be heard.

Enticed by the lure of
diamond and pearls,
looking for the prestige
inside their world.

I was setup to be a fool, in a
scheme to lose.

Framed, by those with a
bogus claim. Manipulated
to fail. The devil is in the
details.

"Betrayal"

QUEEN BEE

"Queen Bee," a lovely display
for the eyes to see. Buzzing
about the day, in a
very
special way.

She flew into my world,
dressed in scarlet attire,
wearing yellow
diamonds,
and black pearls.

She took a beeline, straight
for my heart. In a moment
of time, a love affair
was about to start.

With a jolt from her sting
she took control of my
mind, full of love
my
heart went blind.

Queen Bee, like a sweet
blossom on a redbud tree,
so is she.

Her face glows beneath a
soft honeycomb light.
warming my heart
in
the shadows of night.

A kiss from her lips,
comes the taste of
sweet honey drips.
She dances with the spring
flowers. To music of rosebuds,
that flourish beneath
the rain showers.

Queen Bee, the world gave
her to me. She takes care
of all my needs. No
one can intercede.

The love of my life, she
is a good thing. With magic
of a gentle sting, she
makes my heart sing.

Her world is coated with honey.
only my eyes can see.
she is my Queen Bee.

With her soft tender charm
I am delighted,
my heart is excited.

Queen Bee, happy as can be,
sitting beneath a
green apple tree.

A sweet taste of honey,
for her I spend all my
money, she belong to me,
happy in love, so are we.

"The Queen Bee"

NOT A GOOD DAY TO DIE

Mired in combat, under heavy
attack, in the jungle of warfare.
Enduring pain that had overcome
me, and danger that had befriended
me.

Still living was on my mind, it was
not a good day to die. Only by the
grace of God, do I survive.

The enemy had come to take me
out, I had not a single doubt.
Invading my space, fire and light
were blazing up the place, they were
trying to shorten my days.

My pain was such that I could only
cry, but despite my burden I would
fight to survive. It was a time to live,
not a good day to die.

Pumping rounds, the enemy came
to cut me down.

Bullets ricocheting of the jungle
wall, I thought my life was at a lost.

Exploding bombs in the night. I
learned how to put up a hard fight.

Running through the battle field
of life, where men hearts are colder
then ice.

Ash and smoke blacken the sky,
my eyes beheld an angel standing
nearby, it was not a good day to die.

With wings on my feet, my soul
raced again retreat, my mind fought
again defeat.

My blood have been spilled,
running through the jungle of life's
battle field.

A fight for victory, faith I was led to
try. My fears I tried to hide. Only
by the grace of God, do I survive.

"It was Not a Good Day to Die."

COME ALIVE

Come alive, like the
crystal blue
sky.

In the world of
sweet apple
pie.

Open your eyes. Blossom
to life like a
flower.

Feel the gentleness
of the rain
showers.

Come alive oh, sky.
Let my eyes
behold a
smile.

Come alive like
the morning
sun.

Like the deer that
leap and
run.

Let your dreams
blossom with
the radiant
sunshine.

In the prime of your time,
with rhythm
and rhyme.

Come alive with wings to
fly. With words
to inspire.

Like the stars that
come out
to play.

After a beautiful
sunshine
day.

Open your eyes to hope
and dreams, that
flows like a
stream.

come alive oh, night. Like
the blue diamonds
that sparkles
abright.

Carry the moon upon your
Back, across the
rivers and
streams.

Over the mountains to
the early morning
sunbeam.

Come alive when the
night is ripe for
romance.

Take a stroll in
the soft
sand.

Put on the sunshine,
leaving the rain
behind.

In the prime
of your
time.

"Come Alive"

STEEL TRAP

From the sea they came, aboard a gigantic ship that was equipped with a holding cell, shackles, and chains.

Men with evil eyes, and huge size, with blood on their hands. Ruled by a two fisted dictating man. A wicked tyrant enlisting his savage ways of surviving. Smuggling human cargo. Across the ocean's flow.

From the land of Bat Island, inhabited by the Battians people. They came for slaves, sailing the high sea, out of the distant days.

Across the hostile waters, plowing through stormy weather, massive tides, and rolling waves. They came to an unfamiliar place. Searching for strong slaves.

They landed on the seashore near a village where the inhabitants ran free, as far as the eye can see.

Where men and women went through the day, working the fields, and mills. While the children were in school, or at play.

The Battians smugglers waited for the fall of night. When they thought the time would be right.

Soon after dusk, during the dim part of twilight. The Battians men lowered their rafts from the huge ship into the water. Slowly and quietly they came ashore.

They were heavily armed, creeping about the dirt roads, and nearby farms.

They had the look of rugged men. Their skin was rough like brown leather, their hands were stout and hard, they were the Battians armed guards.

They went through the days, wearing berets upon their heads. They didn't look much like soldiers, but killers in stead.

Their uniforms were badly worn. Wearing trousers that were soiled and torn. Dressed as Battians soldiers, doing the job they were chosen.

They carried swords on their sides, guns they held nearby. Men of tyrannized minds, dragging large nets behind.

They took men from their homes. Used some of the women, then left them along.

Men were dragged from their beds, some were beaten, until they bled.

Jayrod, is my name. I was one of those men, grabbed from behind when I was on my way home. Locked in chains. Other men had already been detained.

I could hear men yelling, and women screaming that this wasn't right. Trying to put up a hard fight.

The Battians men were smugglers, who roamed the sea, looking for land with rich green sites. taking slaves from the nights.

As I was pulled along, I noticed a man climbing out of a grave. He was a grave robber, wearing dead men clothes. A stiff collared white shirt, black top hat, and a black suit, all dirty and old.

He came out of the grave yard onto the road. He was covered with mildew, or mold. The smugglers took him along, he had no home.

We were marched down to the seashore, put in old wooden rafts and carried out to sea to board the awaiting ship. Some men were made to swim, out to the vessel. The smugglers had threaten to shoot them.

We were made to strip down to our shorts, and blindfolded. Thrown into the ship's holding cell. Packed in like a herd of cattle, and sailed of to hell.

We were marked as slaves, for us the smugglers had came, bearing their shackles, and their chains.

"everybody settle down. I don't want no moving around." Yelled the captain. "This ship must stay on course. If any of you fail to cooperate you will be thrown overboard."

The big ship started to move out, plowing through the deep blue sea.

With blindfolds covering our eyes, we could feel the huge ship rocking from side-to-side.

Hear the cracking sound coming from the long hollow vessel. Hear men speaking in foreign tongues, as the big ship moved along. Hear the cry of the seagulls, coming from the area above.

Hours turned into days, days turned into weeks. We were given only raw fish to eat, and food unfit for human consumption, that should have been thrown into the sea, nasty as can be.

Suddenly the ship came to a stop, the anchor was dropped, into the deep water.

Our blindfolds were snatched from our faces. We were brought up to the top deck of the ship, nearing the end of a long slow trip.

My eyes searched for the sun, but there was none. We had arrived in an unknown land, where an escape seemed to have no chance.

Once again we were put into rafts. "Let's go, let's go, get up there you peasants," the evil men shouted.

We took a turn into a narrow river, aligned on both sides by plenty of green small trees, we were unease.

Across the sea on a ship. Now into our final trip. Rain begin to pour into the day, as we made our way.

Herded through the wilderness like wild dogs. Slugging through black mud down a narrow dirt road, moving in droves.

We were on the go, the sun was sinking low. Between the space where day and night clash, and across the sky, the stars had begin to splash.

We had arrived on a hidden island. Long chains bound our hands. Leg irons bound our feet. We were desperate for food to eat.

Men came on horses that wore leather armor flapping across their backs, with guns and whips. Violent words spurted from their lips.

"Alright you maggots, stop dragging along. Pickup the chains, and move on. Anybody messing around, will be shot down."

The Battians men yelled and cursed. The horses kick up mud with their hoofs, as they galloped, pounding the ground, along side of us.

We were brought to a foreign land, to a place called Bat Island. A few miles from the sea. We traveled a road that lies across the mountains, with no one to hear our plea.

The land of a distant tribe, of a previous generation, a lost civilization. Leftover from a fallen empire.

A place, where men were living in rage. A place perhaps removed from the map.

A chunk of the universe that no civilized human being, has ever seen. That lies beyond the windows of the world.

We marched into the city of Zielito. It was like a city of ruin. Enclosed by a high wall, erected with huge wooden logs.

Inside the city stood many tall white tents. The soldiers would visit them to be with their women, or when in need of slumber, or food, often drinking booze.

Iron holding cells lined the right side of the city wall. The tops of the holding cells were covered with long branches of palm trees, that bore faded brown leaves.

Men were locked inside, some were barely alive, staring with desperate eyes. Awaiting daybreak to labor another long hard day, without pay.

At the front of the city stood a huge black cage, near the heavy thick gates that secured the place.

They call it the "Steel Trap." One way in, and no way out. Where men are sent to die, Stripped of most of their clothes once inside.

I could see the half naked men within, and the terror in their eyes, struggling to survive. Like living in hell until the day you die.

Condemned to death by a tyrant that ruled with an iron fist, Clinging to his evil ways, his heart was full of hate. Hiding behind the city walls and tall gates.

The men that were thrown into the Steel Trap, were offered up for a sacrifice to their god.

A ritual that was thought to bring an abundance of live, for the battians people,

I was thrown into the holding cells that lined the right side of the city wall. Where the men would get into brawls, over gambling debts, or picking the wrong place to sit.

The night had passed. The curtains of dawn open wide. The secrets tales of the tribe could not hide.

Revealing a land that was tarnished by the men evil ways. Men that practice the episodes of the evil ancient days.

Dust filled the air from the foot of horses as battians soldiers rode hard and fast, with watching eyes, as they passed by.

The illegal slaves were brought to the land to rebuild the city, and work the fields. Those who refused to labor were thrown into the bowels of the Steel Trap, and later killed.

Slaves were matched against one another in a test of strength, engaging in hand-to-hand combat, for the prize of a cigarette and a strong drink.

The winner was sent back to the holding cell. The loser was thrown into the Steel Trap, and doomed to die, on the night of the full moon , beneath the dark sky.

Men who tried to escape from the island were also thrown into the Steel Trap, and condemned to die, there was no place they could hide.

The Steel Trap was built over the mouth of a cave, a tradition handed down from the Battians ancient days.

In the bottom of the huge black cage lain a door, that led down into the dark cave, from the Steel Trap's floor.

Inside the cave lived what seemed to be a huge animal like man. Half beast, half man, he appeared to be.

The Battians people called him "Romendon." Which meant "Man of Beast." He was gruesome, and believed to be their god, that lived in the days of the fallen empire.

On the night of the full moon. Romendon would come up from his cave, into the Steel Trap, through a door, that lies at the bottom of the Steel Trap floor.

He was big as a giant. His hair grew long like the mane of a lion, about his head, and about is shoulders. Walking on his hind legs most of the time.

Fangs protruded upward from his mouth. Extending up and over his upper lip. He never stood up straight, always bent over from his waist and hip.

He had claws that opened like a switch blade, that easily cut into the flesh of the slaves.

On the night of the full moon, the condemned men would tremble in fear. Some of them were about to be killed.

Inside the Steel Trap, they could hear the howl of Romendon, the Man of Beast, as he rumbled through the cave, at a very fast pace.

They would kneel and pray. Their eyes may never see another day.

"Let's say our late good-byes, for tomorrow some of us will die." proclaimed one of the slaves, as sweat ran down his face.

Suddenly Romendon burst into the Steel Trap, coming up through the trap door, that opens within the floor.

Steam begin to flow in, rising up from the trap door. Flowing in among the condemned men.

Romendon violently grabbed hold on one of them. Played with him like a cat toiling with a mouse, in the basement of an old house before the kill. He was a savage, it was in his will.

Women and men of the Battians people, bowed and cheered whenever Romendon entered the Steel Trap. They chanted his name, "Romendon! Romendon! Romendon!" he was their god, they prided him, and feared him.

He picked the man up, and tossed him over his huge shoulder. Swiftly exiting the Steel Trap, through the bottom of the floor, using the trap door.

On that very same night. Romendon once again returned. Up through the trap door he came, looking for another man.

The slaves scattered about throughout the Steel trap, trying to save themselves from the savage beast, but on this night lives would be lost, at any cost.

He begin growling aloud, antagonizing the men, and taunting them. It was the beast in him.
He grabbed one, threw him over his shoulder.
Down into the dark cave, he raced.

Swiftly he went, leaving behind an unpleasant scent. On the night of the full moon, he often returned soon.

Weeks turned into months, months into years. Men had been killed. I was looking for a way out. Planning an escape, trying to concoct a secret route.

At the end of a grueling day. I managed to loose myself from the chains, that bind my hands. My body had been afflicted with pain.

I broke away. At this point I refuse to stay. I began to run

hard, setting myself apart from the place, that sacrificed men to a beast that lived in a cave.

I made my way down to a cold lake. Vapor was rising from the surface. I was desperate, willing to do whatever it takes, to escape.

I dove in, and started to swim across seeming to be lost. The water was extremely cold, my body began to lose control.

Then the horsemen's came, with their shackles and their chains.

"Seize him, seize him now," one of the horsemen cried out, as the foot of the horses splashed cold water round about.

I was wet and shivering, as the evil men dragged me out. Crocodiles waited near by, I watched them from the depth of my eyes.

"Bring him here," the captain yelled. "How long, was he gone? Fifty lashes with the whip," these words flowed from his lips.

"Throw him into the Steel Trap. At the next full moon perhaps, he will be the next to die, beneath the dark sky.

Time had move on. A bad moon was rising. It was the birth of another full moon, our lives were doomed.

Battians soldiers stood atop the gun towers on watch. It was time for another sacrifice.

We would kneel and pray, for tomorrow would be our last day.

The wind began to blow hard, another sacrifice was about to start. The winter rains had came, falling hard upon the city. Pounding the grounds, as if to lay the city down.

The slaves inside the Steel Trap stood still. A strange mist came upon the city of Zeilito, that only one man could feel.

It had been revealed, that on this dark night, many men would be kill.

Suddenly we heard the growl of Romendon, and the pounding of his footsteps, as he was storming through the cave.

Up through the door, that was built in the Steel Trap floor, he came. Clawing at his blood stained teeth, and showing his fangs. Searching for the right man.

Steam billowed up through the open trap door, from down below.

Again the Battians onlookers bowed and cheered. Chanting the name of Romendon. Each time he came, for a condemned man they would carry on the same.

He stood there, just a few feet in front of the trap door, staring across the floor. Looking from side-to-side, his long woolly hair partially covered his eyes.

He begin to move about, among the men. Within and without. He was a scary sight, it was a horrible night.

In an instant he leaped across the Steel Trap floor, lashed onto my body, and tossed me around.

The other men were afraid, they made not a sound. He let go a loud roar, as he had done before.

He threw me over his shoulder, and stormed down through the open trap door.

Down through the dark cave we went, I could smell his awful scent. I was terrified, tears rolled down my eyes.

Human skulls, and dead men bones were scattered throughout the cave. I could hear the roar of the sea, and the clashing of the waves.

Flames of fire emanated from the huge torches that gave a tongue of light to the place.

He threw me to the ground, and started to wander around, as if searching for something to keep me bound,

In a moment of time, I thought I heard bells ringing, or the tune of chimes.

I turned to look! Coming toward me were three spotted black and white goats, with pieces of shiny metal hanging around their necks and their throats.

Striking together making a loud sharp ringing sound.

The goats appeared to be playful and friendly. I picked myself up from the ground, and begin patting them, stroking my hands across their backs, in a gentle act.

Romendon was not far behind, I was running out of time.

I managed to pull a piece of sharp metal that was fastened to one of the goats, hanging beneath his throat.

I hid it in the palm of my hand, and waited for the Man of Beast. I had a plan, here I would draw the line in the sand.

Out of the darkness he came, running toward me carrying long rusty chains.

He stood right before me. Threw his huge head back, and raised his hairy face toward the sky. Then roared like a lion. Soon I would be dying, so I thought.

He grabbed hold of me, then lifted me up with both hands. I became entangled in the chains.

Suddenly he lowered me back down, to the ground. Thrusting my weak body to the floor of the cave.

He became enraged, angrily staring at me with his big eyes, open wide. I could not run, I could not hide.

He begin to howl aloud, making a powerful noise that echoed throughout the dark cave, I could see the wild beast that was full in his face.

He raised his head high, swiftly moving it around. Beneath his huge foot he kept me pinned down.

In an instant! Romendon, the Man of Beast grabbed hold of my shoulders lifting me high. I could see straight into his big brown eyes.

He pulled me closer to his face, I was amazed of the size of his head, and the size of his eyes. I was petrified.

I reached out with the sharp piece of metal that I held in my hand, in a quest to carryout my plan.

quickly, I took a hard swipe right across his face, cutting into his eyes. I was desperate to save myself from the jaws of the beast, this was the only thing left.

He cried out in pain, loosed me from his hands. Threw me to the ground, making a noisy sound straggling around.

Blood was streaming from his face. I made haste, through the cave I raced.

Leaving Romendon behind, rendering him blind. I wandered about, searching the cave then found a way out. Back to the Steel Trap I went.

I could still smell the bad scent that rubbed off on me from that maniac, when I was attacked.

Up through the door, I emerged from the bottom of the Steel Trap floor.

"Let's go! Let's go," I hallooed, at the brokenhearted men inside. "Come on, hurry up, Let's get out of here," I cried out, as I was running about.

Out of the Steel Trap, we scampered. Quickly moving out through the bottom of the floor, running through the trap door. Making our way outside the city wall, running fast, cutting through the darkness of nightfall.

The Grave Robber was lagging behind, but we were wasting no time.

Tears of joy ran down our faces, as we searched for safe places. To hide away, without delay, from the evil men that would perhaps follow this route. "Come on Grave Robber, run faster," I called out.

The Grave Robber was out of breath barely moving along. He tried to run faster, but stumbled and fell, we all burst out in laughter.

We hid out in the night, in the darkness away from the light. We assembled ourselves near the sea. Plotting our strategy, to set the other slave free.

We returned to the city in the dead of night, when the time was about right. Prepared for a hard fight.

We had become warriors overpowering the gate keepers tying them up with rode, seizing their weapons, now we had hope.

We entered the city from the rear. Digging deep, crawling beneath the back wall. We overpowered the watch guards, and restrained them. It was time for their downfall.

We took their weapons. Into the holding cells we put them all, that aligned the city walls.

Making haste, freeing the other slaves from the belly of their holding cages.

We took horses riding bareback, coming under fierce attack. Grabbing food and supplies, as we continued to ride. Crammed it into sacks moving fast no time for looking back.

The Battians soldiers were awaken. They filed out of their tents with guns, we were on the run. In a quest to reach the sea before the rising of the sun.

Some were wearing long johns, other were struggling to get dressed, we had them running about in a big mess.

They begin blasting rounds, running wild through the city grounds.

Bullets were flying everywhere under the sky, at this point we didn't care if we lived or if we die.

The evil men fell upon some of the slaves with all they had, as we made way down a mountain pass.

A number of the slaves were beaten; shot down by the soldier's gun rounds.

We fired back, fleeing a heavy attack. It was now warfare, fire and smoke fill the air. From a distance I could see the city burning. Heads would roll, but the fleeing slaves would seize control.

We approached the rafts at the edge of the river that led to sea, trying to leave behind the horrible memories.

We let the horses go. In a haste we were trying to reach the tyrant ship that awaits, before the soldiers show.

The Grave Robber once again lagged behind. He was one of a kind, strange and funny at the same time.

I said to him on one occasion that something bad was going to happen, if he didn't stop wearing dead men clothes.

"Ok, Ok," he replied. "What you just said is too tall, to be Short." "What do you mean by that?" I asked.

"These ain't dead men clothes, these is mine clothes, and I ain't dead," is what he said. Then we begin to laugh.

We moved out across the water. Some of us were riding in rafts paddling away, before the start of day, trying to reach the awaiting ship.

It didn't belong to us, but we were going to seize it, to take us across the sea.

To a land where we would rather be. Men were being crucified, we were fighting to stay alive.

Some of the other slave swam out to the ship. A few were killed by the crocodiles, swarming the waters in single files.

A time to live, a time to die. These brave men gave their lives that we may survive.

"May all the men left behind be at rest. They have all done their very best. A farewell, and a good-bye to all that have died."

Finally we reached the awaiting ship, and climbed aboard. The angry sound of evil men that followed could be heard.

They continued to get of rounds. The Grave Robber was shot down as he came out of a small boat, climbing a rope going up the side of the ship.

He plummeted into the deep water, never to make the return trip. "So long to the Grave Robber, his eyes will see no tomorrow, for him I hang my head in sorrow."

It was time to shove off, set sail for home, we had been gone to long.

swarming sharks were looming in the waters below, as the ship started to go.

Swarming like raging bees, as we traveled a marrow stretch of river surrounded by lot of small green trees.

Finally we were sailing the deep blue sea, on a return trip home. A storm was rising, dark clouds covered the ship. Hard rain would soon be arriving.

The sky was angry, the hard rain begin to fall. The waves of the sea grew extremely tall. Like rolling hills, men were struck with fear.

A hard wind was blowing across the sea. The ship went into a dive, we were in a fight to survive.

Not knowing if we would make it out dead, or alive. Only mountains and sky were before our eyes.

Charting our course of direction by night we looked for the brightest star. That shined from a distance, whether near or far.

By day we sailed toward the burning sun, at times there was none.

Slicing through the winds, and rain in the cold of night. Clouds that looked like black oil loomed ahead. The moon refused to give us light, as we held on tight.

It could barely be seen. Hiding behind the night clouds, we tried to keep our minds keen.

Plowing through the hostile waters where the sea opened it's gates. We sailed straight into our fate.

Up ahead was another ship, sailing toward us with heavy artillery, guns of heavy caliber, it was difficult for our eyes to see.

Before long we were fired upon. We sailed as fast as possible. Sailing away into the night. The darkness hid us from the light.

We sailed cold nights, and long hard days. The big ship was climbing the tall waves.

The winds were raging, fiercely blowing. Behind our ship the enemy was chasing.

The waves grew even bigger extending high, like mountains reaching for the sky.

Our ship was tossed about, and blown of course. We got turned around, she was about to go down. Then with our sails set high, she plowed ruggedly through the untamed sea, it was destiny.

The enemy ship got lost in the storm, we used binoculars to gaze around, but she was nowhere to be found.

We journeyed into the next day, for home we were on our way. The morning sun was rising, we were still surviving

We had been dreaming of home, for so very long. Now our eyes had caught the first light of the rising sun.

On this beautiful day the sea seemed to welcome us. Many days we had sailed from morning to dusk, day and night, through the darkness, and through the light.

We tried to follow the planets above, to get back to the ones we love.

We were nearing home sailing the deep blue. Seabirds were flying above, holding green leaves in their beaks that gave us a clue.

Sailing through the open breeze, our minds were now somewhat at ease. Our hearts were very pleased.

At last we were turning for home. We could see flocks of birds feeding on the seashore. Smell the sweet scent of apple blossom and pine, feeling the warm sunshine.

Returning home from beyond the windows of the world, in a hidden land. Where innocent men were slapped with a bogus wrap. Thrust into the Steel Trap.

Where evil men emerged from their fallen empire, clinging to their evil ways, and bloody days. In a land that had collapsed, ripped from the face of the map.

"The Steel Trap"

RUNNING AWAY WITH LOVE

I arise this morning as I ought,
the day shined sunny and bright
as I thought.

into the age of innocence true love
is what I sought. My love, was on
my mind, as we ran in the lanes
of time.

Two lovers in the night,
beneath the splendor of
starlight, that sparkles high above.
"Running Away with Love."

Whisking through the wind,
setting a new trend. At the
close of day, before the twilight
wears away.

Setting love goals the first
day we met. Running to
an oasis that nestles beneath
the sunset.

Too young to know,
the way love is suppose
to go.

Running Away with Love, to the call
of lovely sounds. Hanging on to what
we have found.

Hiding in the night,
bathing in the moonlight.

Chasing lovely dreams,
that blossom like sunflowers
resting beneath the
sunbeams.

Too young to understand, the magic
of sweet romance. Running where
the day is fair, where love
takes to the air.

Running Away with Love, through
the falling snow. Searching for
the right place to go, blending
with the rainbow.

Running among the colors of wild
flowers, under the summer showers.
Into the brilliance of the sunshine,
sweet serenity we seek
to find.

Beyond the mountain rise, where
the eagles flies. To the hills of
nature calls, before the eyes of fall.
Drenched in sunlight, scaling
the heights.

Running Away with Love,
where the air is fresh, and
where love comes
first.

To the flamingo shows, where the
mighty river flows. Where the
pink swans gather in the lakes,
when the early morning
awakes.

Beneath the spring rains, that whisper
across the open plains. Where our
hearts are not dampen
by pain.

Across the rolling meadows,
to the secret places where the
sunshine goes.

Racing with the winds, looking for
hiding places for our love
to blend. Two lovers, running
undercover.

Eloping in the night, when
the stars are bright. From
sunrise to dusk, just the
two of us.

Looking for the zest of life.
soon to become husband
and wife.

Where sparks from the sun paints
the night. Ignited by the falling
stars above.

Creating the wonder of starlight,
making for a beautiful
sight.

"Running Away with Love"

RED HOT BLUE NIGHTS

The sun was sailing across the red sky,
headed for the sunset.

The twilight carried red colors of the
sunset into the night, glowing with the
moon's blue light.

I was cruising through the streets of the
city, the night was very pretty.

People were dancing in the streets,
beneath the red and blue neon
lights, where fun was awaiting, it was
exhilarating.

I was driving kind of slow, with no
particular place to go.

The night air was soft and warm. I could
feel the surge of it upon my skin.

I begin to drive a little faster so that my
face could feel the coolness of the wind.

My short sleeve shirt was moist, slightly
wet. My body was damp with sweat,
that drained from my shoulders, down
across my back, I was feeling relaxed.

The night was sizzling, the red skies had
faded away, into the red sunset at the
end of the day.

Blue light reflected off the moon upon
the hot summer night, painting the
night blue. The colorful stars would join
in too.

It was a magnificent sight, that creating a "Red Hot Blue Night."

I was on a pleasure run, just looking to have a little fun.

I met with friends at a popular night spot, where things got very hot. We laughed and danced, sang along with a local band.

My friends became a wild bunch, getting too intoxicated. Fights broke out, as it was anticipated. Gunshots rang out, round about.

Violent trouble had been started, I quickly departed, headed for home, I was all along.

When the morning came, I grabbed a quick shower, in the early morning hours.

After getting dressed, I got into my vehicle and traveled due west. Headed downtown to a beautiful restaurant for breakfast. Listening to the radio that serenaded the town, with the latest musical sounds.

When I finished, I left a small tip. It was time to hit the highway, and give this place the slip.

I notice a woman standing outside the restaurant near the entrance door, as I started to go.

Upon her face father time, had
sculptured the look of a woman well
past her prime.

The wind, and the sun had took its toll,
it had started to show. Perhaps due to a
life of excessive fun, constantly on the
run.

Maybe alcohol misuse, a street life of
physical abuse, or a woman that seemed
to be on the loose.

She asked me for the time, I complied
with lots on my mind. We begin to talk,
went for a little walk.

She mentioned that she was new in
town, only a few days had she been
around.

Strolling the streets of the city, trying
to find her way. Walking in the warm
sunny day.

I could not ignore that she maintained
a fantastic youthful figure. She caught
my eyes, with a friendly smile, then she
asked me for a ride.

"Could you give me a ride please?"
"Where are you going?" I asked. "Out
to the countryside," she replied.

She spoke with a soft voice, I was just
a boy of nineteen, just coming onto
the scene. Recently out of high school,
trying to be cool, out for a cruise.

It was my first car, I had not driven it very far. Shiny wheels, looking for fun, in the sun. Trying to figure out how I was going to live.

We drove for miles, she seemed to be at peace enjoying the ride to the countryside. I could see the sparkles in her eyes.

We were engaged in an in-depth conversation, it appeared that she was in search of a revelation.

Looking for answers to a problem life, showing signs of an abused wife.

"I will be staying with my sister for a week and a day, I had to get away. So I will be spending a little time here," she said.

"OK," why did you have to get away? If I may."

"I have filed for a divorce, waiting for it to take its course. I am separated, my life has been devastated."

"The man whom I am separated live in San Francisco. He is very abusive, so I had to go," she replied.

Her name was Jan, my name is Ted, up ahead stood a small fruit stand.

We stopped for something cold to drink, and ice cream. The day was relatively warm reflecting rays of bright sunbeams.

Jan gently took my hand, as we strolled toward the fruit stand. She held me in a soft embrace. Her smile begin to light up her face.

She was very playful like a child. Her earrings sent traces of light about her eyes, reflected by the sun, as the world turned.

We set and talked for awhile, a happy pair, lost in the sun glair. Her face gave warmth to the air.

She started to cry, speaking of the hard times she have endured from the hands of her man.

"I would have left him long ago, only if I had the right plan," she tried to explain.

She whispered in my ear, as we took in a breath of

fresh air, telling me how she would love to be my gal, but her husband would never let her be. She asked if I could find a way to set her free.

I didn't answer. I wondered what she meant by that. We had just recently met, I did not really know her as of yet.

We returned to the car. I continued to drive, enjoying the ride, taking leisure in the countryside.

It was a beautiful red sky day, to Jan sister's place we were on our way.

Taking in the scenery, holding fast to a memory. Making stops in between, at sites to be seen.

I open the engine up wide, down the highway we would fly.

The wind blew about her hair, the day was warm and fair.

We took a turn off the highway, pulling into the banks of an undisturbed lake.

There I parked my car, from the main road we were not very far.

The evening sun had climbed high into the day. Upon the green grass beneath the palm trees we would lay. It was as though the red sky, came down to smile.

The lake was mild and crystal clear, this moment gave my heart a thrill. Spending time with Jan, made me feel like a real man.

The lake was one of the prettiest lakes my eyes had ever seen. Like the one in my hometown, that echoes summer sounds. It glitter like gold, a beauty for the eyes to behold.

A kiss, I placed upon her inviting lips,
her eyes insist. One thing led to another,
we took our relationship even farther.

The magic in the air was fully awake.
Soon we would be swimming in the
lake.

Time had wore on. The day was coming
to an end, other fun places we had been.

It had not been very long since we met.
Now we were holding hands, making
plans, gazing into the sunset.

I thought this was the way things were
suppose to be, and so along were we.

Soon another "Red Hot Blue Night"
fell upon the countryside. The crescent
moon gave blue light to our eyes.

Starlight was glowing like sparks in the
night. Everything appeared to be going
just right.

Time seemed to be moving very fast.
Since I got behind the wheel of my car,
lots of time had past.

Finally we pulled into the driveway of
Jan sister's house. Coming in from the
south.

It appeared that all the lights had been
turned off, I seemed to be lost.

I began to feel an uneasiness. The air was hanging heavily over the plain, I thought maybe I should never have came.

It was as though I could feel the darkness touching my skin. Upon the wind the moon seemed to pull. The air rang with the cry of wolves.

We had arrived. There! Jan's man was waiting in the shadows nearby.

He was a large man, out of the darkness he came.

His head was shaven. Through the darkness I could see his hands madly waving. Then came the crying sounds of the ravens.

I had heard that this was the sign of bad luck. If it was so then I was stuck.

What could I do? Across the house the black birds had already flew.

The man rushed to my car, from beneath my seat I grabbed a crowbar.

The night was calm and still. Steam raised from his head, into the night air, his eyes were fiery red.

"Where have you been witch," the man angrily insist.

He abruptly opened my car door on the passage side. I could see the madness in his eyes.

He put his hands on Jan, pulling her from the car into the night air, holding on to her hair.

To me, he was a total stranger, a man filled with anger. He was highly upset, my eyes could plainly see that.

He threw Jan, hard into a stack of trash cans. She was a beauty, he was a beast, I wondered how could this be?

He started to beat her yelling out curse words, that my ears had never heard.

I started to leave, my heart had been deceived. The two were not separated, as I had anticipated.

She was being brutalized, a disgrace before my eyes, my heart bled for her.

The instinct that rested in my mind revealed that I should flee, but I could hear her plea. she cried out in pain, her tears poured like rain.

I began to drive away. It was another "Red Hot Blue Night," and nothing seemed to be going right. The red skies had faded from the day, my lips could not find words to say.

I quickly come to a stop. In a rush, I put my car in reverse. The man continued to beat up on Jan, into the night he cursed.

"Hey, stop hitting her," I yelled. "what you say boy, you go to hell," the man replied. I could see the tears in Jan's eyes.

I thought there was nothing I could do, but before she die, I must try.

Things had got really hot, like coals that burn beneath a steel pot.

He continued to strike her with both hands. I failed to understand, she seemed to be such a gentle woman, and he such a brutal man.

I had heard that opposite attracts, but this could not be exact.

I exited the vehicle, and grabbed him by the neck in an attempt to pull him off Jan. He was a very strong man.

He turned around, knocking me to the ground. With his powerful muscular strength, he caught me with a punch, across my car I was sent.

Suddenly I felt his big boot on my throat, I was being choked.

A kick in the head, I was in pain, I laid on the ground and bled. Soaked in blood, my trousers were tore, my body was sore.

I could feel the excruciating pain surge
through my bones. He struck me hard, I
was left wandering in the dark.

Out of the corner of my bloodshot eyes,
I could barely see Jan. She had a faraway
look in her eyes.

She grabbed my crowbar from the car,
hitting the man on side of his head,
knocking him down to the ground.

He was out cold. She went into his
pockets taking the money from his
billfold.

"Let's get out of here," I said, as the man
laid and bled with blood gushing from
his head.

"No," she said. "I want him dead. Then
you will be my man if you are not
afraid," she spoke in a soft sweet voice.

She retrieve a pearl handle revolver
from her purse and handed it to me.
My hands were shaking, I had been
forsaken.

"Shoot him Ted, shoot him now," she
cried out in a loud voice. "You want me
don't you? Don't you?

I was lost for words, and refused to go
along. No way would I kill that man
I knew this was wrong. She had been
abused, but I was being misused.

She had picked me like a cherry, her
man she wanted to bury.

She had approached me without any
fear, hoping to have the man killed.

Like a fool I had been played. She had
learned to play the game well, during
her street life days, that's impressed
upon her face.

I felt that I was not the first, she carries
the revolver in her purse. I was misled,
she wanted her husband dead.

Suddenly she pull a knife! Plunging it
into his side, in the wink of an eye.

She wickedly pulled the gun from my
hand, as the man laid on the ground,
pumping three rounds, into his
forehead. Bang! Bang! Bang! there he
bled, he laid dead.

I was stunned. Racing through her veins
was the cold blood of a killer. Blood that
spattered all across her face, during her
time of rage.

She carried the knife down to the creek
with blood on her hand, and buried
it in the sand. Placed the pearl handle
revolver back into her purse.

I was petrified. Nothing could be worst,
I could not say very much.

She washed away the bloodstains from
her hands. Boarded the late night
greyhound, leaving town. That was the
last time I seen the likes of Jan.

Not ever did I hear a word about the
death of that man, I didn't even know
his name.

Memories of that horrible night still
lingers in my mind, haunting my soul
most of the time.

I am much older now. Been married
and divorced. My life has been set on a
rocky course.

I have children of my own, but I live
along. At times I travel from city-to-city
looking for a different places to roam.

I find it hard to hold down a steady job,
at times struggling not to starve. Jan and
the man, I failed to understand.

I still recall, the memories of it all.
The fights, and the lights, that burned
bright. Lighting up the nights. Jan and
the man, who can understand.

"Red Hot Blue Nights"

HANGING ONTO THE WIND

Hanging onto the wind, as long
as I can. Going on a wild
Ride, learning ways
To fly.

Sailing over the mighty hills,
Above the open fields.
Through the cool
Atmosphere.

Looking for a way the unwind,
From the effects of hard
Times. Slicing through
The air, with no
Time to spare.

Into the depth of solitude,
Searching for the
Right path to
Choose.

Hanging onto the wind, high
Above the sky. Soon I
will descend. Before
The day comes
To an end.

Listening to the clanging of
Silver chimes. Waiting
To hold you in
My arms.

Flying across rivers and
Lakes, before
The twilight
Awakes.

Through twist and turns, on
A sky diving run. Shades
And shadows, shields
My soul from
The sun.

Zooming over the land of
Tall trees. To the
Flashing waves of
roaring seas.

The water was delightful,
And warm. Aligned
By trees of evergreen
And palm.

Sailing across the flaming
Desert. To the coolness
Of the seashore. Over
Rolling tides,
Learning how
To stay
Alive.

Hanging onto the wind, flying
Across forgotten memories,
Buried in the ashes of
Time. To the skies
Of serenity, to
Renew my
Mind.

To the stars of heaven,
That give light
To my soul.

Hearing sweet love song, rising
From the days gone cold.
Flying in the shiny
Nights of
Gold.

Hanging onto the wind, over
The valley of burning
Flames. It will bring
Me back again, to
the doors of my
Domain.

Zooming across the ocean blue.
Reflecting blazing trailing
Lacing the air, where
Song birds once
Flew. Bringing
Love songs
To me and
You.

Gliding up stream, where
The fresh water flow
Into the meadows.
Cooling the heat
Of the sunlight
Beams.

Hanging onto the wind, trying
Not to fall for sin, or into
A world of crime. No
Peace will
I find.

Trying to retrieve love from
The sky. That has melted
Into the years
Gone
By.

Hanging onto the wind, an old
Familiar friend. Blowing
Kisses with a smile,
Sliding across
The open
Sky.

To a place where life is not
A cheap thrill. Where
Life is filled with
Love that my
Heart can
Feel.

Hanging onto the swirling
Wind, sweet air upon
My skin. soon I
Will return
Again.

"Hanging Onto
The Wind"

LAW DOGS

The city was in an uproar. Violent crime was tearing through the streets like a deep sore.

Running rampant like blood gushing from an open wound, with no way to stop the bleeding. Men were gunned down for no reason.

A government agency was created to cleanup this awful mess. A job like this is in need of only the best.

I am agent-9, A fighter of crime. A hard fight is what I like, trying not to get whacked.

I was called upon to join the team, along with my two partners, agent-10, and agent-11 who burst upon the scene. We were activated to Infiltrate this hell hole, take out the garbage and put it on hold.

Three men fighting hard crime, putting our lives on the line. Men with brave hearts. Men who won't fall apart.

To hell, and back we have been. In the bloody world of crime we know how to win.

We call ourselves the "Law Dogs." Men with a cause, who rise but never fall. A code name given to us by the FBI, working as undercover guys.

Activated to crime infested cities and towns, to bring the violent criminals down.

To cleanup the streets where anything goes; where killers have taken control.

Where crimes, and corruption are deeply ingrained, and the law is turned upside down, with no sense of right, or wrong. Good men have packed up, and gone.

In this case we were activated to a city where men and women were living in fear. Innocent blood was constantly spilled; lawmen and citizens had been killed.

The cry of plea could be heard, across the world. The night air was drenched in cold blood.

People were dragged from their homes and beaten. Others were wrongfully tossed in jail, given water to drink, and only bread would be eaten.

Women would hide, stay home and cry. They were afraid to go out into the streets, overrun by men of deceit. They were made to feel as if they did not belong. Day in, and day out, they would weep and mourn.

Violent men would roam the streets having their way. Those good men who tried to fight back were brutally killed. Others were manipulated by the act of fear.

This was a city where criminals would go to hideout. Holding citizens hostage, making them do without. A city where men would do anything to survive, fighting one another to stay alive.

These men were terrorist. Men who had been found guilty. To evaded there punishment they would flee, refusing to go to jail, leaving a violent trail. Running from the law, persuading witnesses to forget what they saw.

Some had been condemned to die, for them nothing was left, but to die a quick death.

The lives of citizens were impact by violent crime, fear, and deceit. This was the criminal ticket to easy street.

Exposing their evil ways, men and women were enslaved, made to labor long hard days, in positions that never pays.

Law Dogs, standing tall. fighting for one, fighting for all. Came to town, to shut this outrage down.

We knew the job would be rough, we were drilled to be tough. A time to live, a time to die. A time for the enemy to say their last good-bye.

We rolled into the city on point, riding three deep, in a military humvee. Rocket launchers and machineguns were mounted on top. We were rolling in an armor vehicle that is very hard to stop.

We had access to ready artillery, before the midnight hour, packing heavy firepower.

We were on the lookout, for the Mohard brothers, who had snuffed out innocent lives, and ruined others.

We had been warned, that these men were cold
blooded killers. Showing no mercy, not even
a little. In a short span of time, ways to bring
them down emanated from our minds.

The Mohard brothers spotted our humvee
rolling into town. They began shooting out
streetlights, in a move to slow us down.

We rolled in hard, well aware that trouble was
about to start. We dug in for a fierce fight. In an
instant we were blazing up the night.

Hails of gunfire was flying past our heads like
fireballs falling from the sky. The town folk
would run and hide, looking to survive.

Our vehicle was riddled with bullets, as we
rolled over barricades, at a very fast pace.

Crashing past automobiles that were blocking
the streets with no time to waste.

Men were yelling kill, kill. Our blood they were
aiming to spill.

Smashing through fences and walls, now it was
time for the evil giant to fall.

We were involved in a bitter conflict, but we
were men of courage, men that wouldn't quit.

From our humvee we fired rocket propelled
grenades, blowing up a crime infested place,
where the enemy were enraged. Fire burned
high, reaching for the sky, men would die.

Our motto was “never retreat, death before defeat.”

We would not back down , pumping rounds, looking to bring law and order to the town.

Men laid dead in the street, but our mission was not complete.

We forged ahead where thieves occupied the police station, overseeing the illegal day-to-day operation.

Living off others were their way of life. Rulers of the street, engulfed with strife. Packing the heavy guns,

that sent men on the run.

Bold and mean, when we arrived on the scene, setup to take us out, barricading our escape route.

Suddenly we had fought our way to main street, using our imagination. It was time to take back the police station. The terrorist had took it over by force, and barricaded the doors.

Parasites raiding the city streets. Feeding on fears, no one wants to be killed. The situation was severe.

“Hey you in there, throw out your guns, and come out with your hands in the air. There is no time to spare,” the enemy had been warned.

“If you want us, come in, and get us. If you are so tough,” replied the men inside.

Once again our armor humvee was hit by hard fying bullets. We returned fire, unleashing a rocket propelled grenade. Fire begin to burn into the place.

The building went up in smoke, leaving the enemy without hope. This battle was over, we had no doubt. The enemy was buried in fire. We had no other choice, but to take them out.

The Law Dogs existed the vehicle to survey the site. Fire and smoke billowed in the night.

We tried to find a place to lay low, and relax, but there was no place to go. We had no time to spare, only to watch our backs.

Up from behind men were approaching fast, branding their weapons.

Their faces were covered with hoods and mask. At the moment we could not reach our humvee, but we would not be out classed.

With automatic machineguns, and assault weapons they begin to unleash load of firepower, spanning the midnight hour.

The sky was angry. Dark clouds were setting low, we were on the go. The stars disappeared from the night. The moon refrained from shinning light. Lightning strikes, refused to holdback.

The law Dogs, were setup to fall, trying to make the right call. Taking cover behind cars and trucks, running out of luck.

Incoming bullets ricocheted off the building walls. The enemy refused to take a pause, gunning for the Law Dogs, in a quest to kill us all.

Hard rain was pouring into the city. We were slugging through water and mud, the enemy showed no pity.

The cry of the wild could be heard. Out of the line of fire we move away. It was a hard fought battle, but we were in it to stay.

Constantly fired upon. The streets were wet, making it hard to get set. At this time we were unable to reach the vehicle where our powerful weapons were kept.

To get out alive, we used the bandoleers strapped over our shoulders, and across our chest, hosting a chain of ammunition, with the weapons we packed on our sides.

The enemy was elusive, but we had strategic plans to weed them out. Whether dead, or alive, we had no doubt.

The streets were flooded with rain. We got soaked when it came. No time to put on raingear, it was time to kill, or be killed.

Hot lead was falling near us like the pouring rain, I took a bullet in my hand.

One of my Law Dog partners, agent-11, was gunned down, took three rounds in the back, we were under heavy attack.

Gunned down, by an assault rifle round. Shoot to kill, only two of us now live.

"So long to you my Law Dog friend. May you be at peace, now that your life is at an end."

"My eyes will cry for you, tears of stone, for a heart that was strong. The tears in my eyes, say my last good-bye."

Only two of us were left alive, agent-9, and agent-10. We had to fight even harder to survive, but we were in it to win. Running through the muddy streets, combat boots on our feet.

In an instant a black SUV, was speeding straight toward us through the hard rain. My eyes could barely see.

We started to blast round from the guns that we had, the enemy was mad. Bang! Bang! Bang! Shots rang out. We took out the wheelman. He was driving through the rain, with gun in hand.

Out of the SUV others bailed. We were right on their trail. Our lives were at stake, we were destined to take them out, for the town people sake.

The gun battle ensued, we were determined not to lose. Engaged in a hard fight, rain continue to fall upon the night.

Men felled and bled, some took rounds to the head. Drenched across the rain soaked ground they laid dead.

My only partner was agitated, holding me responsible for the death of our fallen comrade. This was far from my imagination, we were caught in a bad situation.

He punched me in the face, I was stun, knocked into a daze. In excruciating pain, earlier I was shot in the hand.

I was already hurt, now I was on the ground eating dirt.

The enemy was tearing through the streets, looking for ways to take us down to defeat.

They assembled themselves, for human life they had no cares.

My partner and I found our way back to the humvee,

where it was filled with high tech weaponry.

The enemy was storming toward us. Leaving their tracks in the mud. Boots on the ground were all we heard.

They unleashed heavy loads of firepower from their artillery. Refusing to letup. We were drinking from a bitter cup.

We were along, the battle was on. Under attack, back-to-back, no time to relax.

Battling through the rain showers, we displayed superior firepower. Blazing up the night, engaged in a hard fight.

We got off more rocket propelled grenades, blowing up the place. A battle ground site, fire and smoke surged into the night.

Citizens joined in, men were gunned down, in an attempt to turn the lawless streets around. Finally the city was returned to the people. The enemy was brought down.

Hired to cleanup the city streets. The Law Dogs were relentless, refusing to be beat. The enemy had gone down in defeat.

It was our job to keep safety and peace flowing. To remain undercover without anyone knowing.

We must be moving on. Not absolute to where we will be going. Working round about. There are other evil men that must be taken out.

Wherever we roam danger awaits. It comes with the territory, this we anticipate.

At times it gets rough, I feel that I have had enough, but someone has to get the job done, to many evil men are still on the run.

I put my life on the line, night and day, no time to play, just fighting crime. Sometimes I'm a prisoner in my own mind.

The woman that I love, left me long ago. Stating that she could not take it anymore. She would constantly cry, afraid that I might soon die.

Maybe in some dark alley, or some lonesome town. Bleeding in the street, or maybe washed up in a creek.

Most of the time I was gone, far away from home, she would be left all along. Working undercover, is filled with troubles. No matter how I tried, certain things would turnout wrong.

In this line of work there are too many ways to die. At anytime your partner can lay dead right by your side. Your life can take a turn, and pass you by.

I was born to track down killers, thieves, and other evil criminals, bring them in, or put them down. Bringing safety and peace to a lawless town.

To conquer, and not be conquered, by men on the run,

or those who are toting illegal guns.

We adopted a unique line of defense against unexpected attacks. Keeping an awareness of the cold hard facts. Having keen eyes to watch our backs.

Taking the enemy out, to be exact.
With no time to relax.
"Law Dogs." Standing tall. Fighting for one,
fighting for all.

ONE MAN BAND

He is a "One Man Band," greeting
the dawn with song and dance.

Standing on street corners telling
gripping tales. Traveling from place
to place leaving behind secret trails.

He journeyed from afar, blowing
a harmonica, and playing a guitar.
Spending lots of time in a dark
whiskey bar.

Wailing about life's struggles in
which he takes part. Telling stories of
love, betrayal, and broken hearts.

As magic in the sky, his songs
seems to come alive. Like the living
memories that glows in his eyes.

Beneath the howling moonlight, he
wails to the spirits in the night.

Never becoming renown, or world
famous, at times playing before a
house of strangers.

Singing in the streets of the dead,
where brave men refuse to tread.

Taking his songs from old secret
places, and from the shadows of
obscured faces. Singing of hard
times, mixed with rhythm and
rhymes.

He reminisces of a lost love one, like
the rising sun, till the night is done.

Lost in music, lost in song, since his
love has gone.

Decades of laughter and pain are
etched on his face, taken from the
pages of his yesterdays.

Bearing testimony to the capacity of
a rough life, and the memories of an
estrange wife.

Caught in a blizzard of loneliness, his
heart is in an awful mess, apart from
his days of happiness.

Singing songs about the love he now
misses, and thoughts of wasted kisses.
The affairs of his heart, that has been
ripped apart.

A One Man Band, drawing young
lovers out beneath the streetlights.
Serenading a host of onlookers well
into the night.

Colorful memories flickers before his
eyes, echoing his love that has slowly
died.

In the habit of losing sleep, his heart
is forever weak.

His pain cannot be concealed, crying
a river of tears, amplifying the way
he feels.

Drinking wine most of the time.
Chain smoking cigarettes. His heart
bleeds, for a woman love that did not
succeed.

He plays his music, and sang his
songs on the sidewalks, and at
storefronts in the dying hours of the
day, then he slips away.

Each song holds secret meanings,
that touches a heart of tears. Taken
from the window of his yesteryears.

His head was once filled with
beautiful dreams, that died like an
old love scene.

pumping out the magic of song,
trying to unlock the past. Looking
for the kind of love he once had.

coming with a unique dance.
Choosing the city streets for a
bandstand.

Strumming his guitar with songs of a
broken heart, for the pleasure of his
fans. Living on the edge of romance.

"The One Man Band"

FALLING IN LOVE AGAIN

Falling in love again,
At spring near
Summer's
End.

Starting all over,
Wishing upon
A four leaf
Clover.

Waiting for autumn to
Descend, setting
A new trends.

Fading cloudy days,
Blue skies before
My face.

Embracing new romance,
Strolling in the
Sands.

Two hearts take to
The winds, let's
Fall in love
Again.

A new sunrise, a
Glow in your
Eyes.

Dancing on a laidback
Afternoon. The
Stars will sing
A new
Tune.

On the night of
The silver
Moon.

Where shall we go from
Here? rising to a new
Atmosphere.

My heart sings, with
The new love
You bring.

Complete with a
Diamond
Ring.

Greeting the early
Morning sunrise,
With a dance.

Holding your
Soft Gentle
Hand.

Beneath the moon, wild
Flowers will
Bloom.

Hearts of two,
Singing
A new
Tune.

Song birds returning to
Spring, fluttering
Their wings
Beginning
To sing.

Chasing the sunset,
Memories of
The day we
Met.

Beneath the winter winds,
Gazing at the rainbow
As we did
Way back
When.

Starting a new beginning,
For the love that
Fell Short of a
Storybook
Ending.

"Falling in Love Again"

THE TRADE HOUSE RIP OFF

The evening was late, the sun had begin to fade; night would be coming soon. Bringing with it, the light of the howling moon, in full bloom.

I was staying at the flamingo hotel, 107 was the number to my room.

My name is Trio, my partner's name was Kurt. We were going over our plans and checking our weapons, getting ready for the big dance, where diamond sparkles like the stars, and money was plentiful like in a dream.

In a short period of time we would be arriving on the scene. Where big wheels from across the nation come to trade business ideas, and strategize how to scam money from anyone, under the sun.

Where men throw their hats into the political arena, and pickup ways to have a successful run.

We would be penetrating an upscale neighborhood. Our destination, "The Trade House."

Where clientele pay up to five-hundred dollars to attend the Trade House Ball, and up to three-hundred dollars to get invited to high fashion events that take place during the summer months, and at the start of fall.

The men who operated this place were on the take, storing all their undisclosed assets in a airtight vault inside the Trade House.

Protected by heavily armed guards who were just waiting for blood to spill, and men to kill.

I had recently been paroled from the pen, doing time, for a bogus crime, paying for my sins. A crime that I would never commit, yet I was locked up in a bottomless pit.

The parole officer had a hand in my early release. His name was Will Cocks, his persuasive influence had a very long reach.

The condition in which the parole had been granted, was deadly.

I, along with my partner, was to takeout the guards at the Trade House. Anyone else who tried to stop us would be smashed. Our job was to rip off the diamonds and take all the cash.

The crooked parole officer would receive sixty percent, and I would keep forty percent, this is how the deal went.

Failure to do so meant life behind bars for me. Sent back to the pen, all over again.

It was a no win situation, but I would rather be on the outside dining with beautiful women rolling in fancy cars, then spending my entire life behind bars. I agreed to do the job.

The parole officer had a twisted mind, holding my freedom hostage till I commit the crime.

I was under duress, given no other alternative to free myself. If I was going to carry out this heist, I would have to be at my very best.

I refused to go back behind prison walls, during hard time, with no life at all.

There were people inside the pen, that would make sure that I never hit the streets again.

Down the expressway we went, my partner and I, in route to the Trade House. I was still angry about the wrongful prison time I had already spent.

Some of the men that were in charge of the Trade House had me incarcerated, during the trial I was manipulated. they were responsible for my conviction. This was their gold and their prediction.

This job meant more to me than just the freedom, and the money. In relation to those men, it meant sweet revenge.

We parked our vehicle in a dense wooded area, at the rear of the targeted site, ready for a hard fight.

We quickly made our way to the Trade House, slogging across a rain soaked field, coming up from the rear. Getting bogged down at times, keeping an open eye. Making sure no one come up from behind.

We came upon three rottweilers that occupied the backyard. They begin to bark. Their mouths were opened wide dripping with slime, ready to tear us apart.

Kurt, quickly pitched two, or three pounds of ground beef in their direction, it was for our protection.

Suddenly there was a hush. The dogs variously attacked the meat then began to eat, we moved across the backyard light on our feet.

Then we went to work, disabling the alarm system, crawled inside the house through a bathroom window.

Dropped down to the hardwood floor, keeping our bodies low.

Wearing knit caps with a pull down mask covering our faces, moving about looking in secret places.

We could hear laughter coming from the bottom floor. It appeared that the guests were having a goodtime, as we watched from behind an upstairs door.

Men and women were commingling, cheerfully moving around. If this thing had gotten out of hand someone would be put down.

In an instant things got rough. Four heavily armed guards burst in, like a whirlwind. Coming in through the front door, on the bottom floor.

Dressed down in riot gear, tinted glass shields on their helmets covering their eyes. Somebody was about to die.

"Someone is in the house! You, search upstairs, you go right, you all come with me, and shut off the lights," the lead guard shouted out, people begin to scream and scatter about.

Out came the weapons. Semiautomatic rifles, pump action shotguns. Some men pulled their pistols firing at will, it were us they were trying to kill.

Bullets begin to fly, people looked for places to hide. Women got caught in between, the Trade House became a chaotic scene.

My partner and I started to fire back, we had come under a deadly attack.

Smoke fill the rooms; the smell of gunpowder lingered in the air. The sound of the guns could be heard, when the battle occurred, carried into the night by the winds. I thought it would never end, how long had it been?

We managed to put down three of the four security guards, they had been pouring it on heavy and hard, right from the start.

Upstairs in the shadows stood another man. He begin firing shots to spoil our plans, from the dark corner where he chose to stand.

He took a bullet in the chest. His body fell from the balcony to the bottom floor, from the look in his eyes he appeared to be obsessed.

We quickly moved downstairs and seized control. "Ok everybody drop to the floor, move in tight and stay close," Kurt demanded, moving back and forth, in a fast stroll.

I could see that he had the heart of a killer beating beneath his chest. His facial expression never change, always remained the same. To him this was just a silly game.

"Is anyone else in the house? Speak up, I can't hear you," Kurt shouted.

"No, no," someone said, as the people inside the Trade House appeared to be shaken and scared.

"Go search the upstairs again Trio." "Ok, hold on." I went upstairs and searched around, I spotted no one. Then from the top of the stairs, I yelled down. "No one is up here," as Kurt was looking up at me with his killer eyes.

"Alright, Alright. Who is going to show me where the money, and the jewelry are stashed?" He asked.

"Hey you, security. Take me to the stuff if you want to stay alive, big guy." Kurt then begun to curse.

The goods were buried inside a wall. We busted through the wall, and took it all. Some two-million dollars in cold hard cash, behind the wall that got smashed.

Loads of jewelry that glitters in the night, like the river that glitter under the moonlight.

"Let's roll Trio. Come on let's go, grab the bags," said Kurt. "Everybody stay put, down on the floor, like I told you before."

Into the night we fled. I got behind the wheel of a car parked out front, and away we sped.

Down the open road we would fly, racing beneath the black sky.

In an instant two speeding cop cars rolled upon us with the siren blasting, and red lights flashing,

I was not about the pull over, I sped up putting the paddle to the metal.

The cops started shooting. A shot took out my back windshield. The wheels began to squeal. In this high

speed chase someone was about to be killed.

Kurt crawled into the back seat. He began pumping rounds, with an assault rifle. Trying to put them down.

One of their cars veered off the road, flipping upside down bursting into flames, for us these men had came.

Suddenly two shots ring out, from the two guns that remained.

Bang! Bang! Kurt had been fatally hit. He went down, stretched across the spattered glass that covered the back seat, we was under lots of heat.

"Kurt, Kurt, are you alright," I cry out in a loud voice, but got no reply, it was a time to die.

Death had befell him, he had been put down, never making another sound.

I bided him a farewell, his eyes will never see another prison cell. death is his freedom.

The cops continued to get of rounds. Slamming their patrol car hard into the back of my vehicle, I continued to drive. They tries to go around, but I refused to let them go by. Blocking their way, each time they sway.

Through the reflection of my rearview mirror my eyes could see that these men were not cops. I remember their faces, from familiar places.

They moved up next to me in a parallel position, slamming into the side of my vehicle.

Debris obscured my vision, causing me to have a collision. Forced off the road into muddy ground, landing upside down.

I could smell gas fumes coming from the fuel line. In a moment of time it burst into frames.

I was felling woozy, but I struggled to crawled out, dragging my aching body across the rough terrain.

Fire and smoke raised in the night, burning bright, above the crash site.

There I lay, barely able to move when two men approached. Standing above me brandishing their weapons taking no prisoners.

They disguised themselves as cops, but they were ex-cons who had been sent to take us out. They grabbed all the money bags, and everything we had.

The last thing I remember is seeing flames exploding from the barrel of a gun, I could not run.

I had been pistol whipped, shot in the head, and left for dead.

I came to my senses hours later when the men had gone. Found myself laying in a pool of blood, left all along.

I had been stuck in the middle of hell, by the power of the parole officer. The men got what they came for. They took the jewelry and the money. It was not a good day, my sunshine had melted away.

They were phony cops. Who worked for the scheming parole officer, Will Cocks. They were mad, took every thing we had, and sped away, working for big pay.

Will Cocks never intended to follow through with his original plan, or do what he had said. I had been setup for a ripped off. He wanted me dead, had a bullet put in my head.

The bullet merely grazed my skull. I struggled to stand on my feet, feeling kind of weak.

Then I began to move out across the rough terrain, getting bogged down in the mud. My clothes were drenched in blood.

Staggering about in search of the main highway. The early morning sun begin to climb atop the day.

My mind was in disarray, my body was racked in pain, I knew who was to blame.

I stumbled into a deep waterhole. I had to fight with snakes to get myself out. The water sent my body shivering cold.

Finally I reached the highway. I watched as a convoy of huge semi trailed trucks went by. One came along and gave me a ride.

"Jump in," the driver said. "You look like something just came up from the dead. What in the world happy to you?" I open my mouth, but could not speak, words would not come out, as I climbed into the seat.

"Hold on, and strap yourself in. I have a heavy load, ready to hit the road. Time is money, and money is gold, let's roll," proclaimed the truck drivers.

As time moved on, My wounds healed. The two men who took the money and jewelry had been killed, by bona fide police officers. Cops that were on the real.

I received word that the parole officer was at the marina, awaiting the arrival of a boat to take him out of the city.

I quickly got into my car, and sped off in that direction. I could see the harbor as I exit the freeway, glowing with orange, and yellowish lights. I was strapped, ready for a fight.

The world of the parole officer was about to crumble, and come to an end. I was racing in the wind.

The moonlight rays were left dancing upon the lake. I moved in quickly before it was to late.

I worked my way out to the docks. There Will Cocks stood, in the shadows away from the harbor lights, holding a briefcase.

I called out his name, "Will Cocks." He quickly turned his head around, recognizing my face.

I could see that he was surprised, by the stare in his eyes. He started to run, then suddenly pulled a gun.

He spun around, quickly getting off three rounds. Bang! Bang! Bang! I dropped down, falling to the dock.

I retrieved my weapon and returned fire. Bang! Bang! Firing twice, he had a heart as cold as ice.

He continued to run, jumped into a speedboat holding onto the briefcase. Down through the lake he raced, barreling across the waters.

I was only seconds behind, grabbed the fastest boat that I could find. Down the lake I went, making good time.

I began to close the gap between the two boats, he twist his body around, still trying to shoot me down.

My boat swiftly plowed through rough waters and waves that splashed from the rear of his vessel.

I could feel the salt water beating upon my face. Burning into my eyes in a dead heat race.

His gun fell silent, no more shells in the chamber. It was a time to survive, or a time to die.

Suddenly his boat veered out of control, bailing out of the waters onto dry ground. Landing on the woody side of the lake, shutting him down.

His body tumbled into the weeds, he scrambled for his briefcase crawling on his knees.

I jumped from my boat in a hurry, my heart was filled with worry.

Will Cocks begin running though the weeds, stumbling and falling, making his way around the trees.

I gave case, running through the rough terrain, and through the trees. Smacked in the face by hanging branches saturated with leaves.

I closed in on him within striking distance. With one big leap I dove onto his back, like a hungry lion bringing down it's prey with a swift attack.

Down to the ground he went, breating hard and heavy. Uttering swearing words, I didn't understand what he had said. I begin to speak instead.

He grabbed the gun from my waist. We fought violently for it, I was in a daze. In an instant the gun discharged. Bang! The bullet struck him round about the heart, ripping his chest apart.

There he laid dead, I was bloody and battled. I needed rest, but had no time to waste. I could hear the cops coming at a fast place.

I took the briefcase and scampered away, running toward tomorrow, out of a world of sorrow.

I recovered more then my shell of the money taken from the Trade House Rip Off, but for the jewelry someone else had taken it all.

Years have passed me by. In the outside world I have found a way to survive.

Never went back to the pen, living on blood money asking to be forgiven for my sins.

I will never be free. Living on the outside looking in. wandering will my life ever be the same again.

I'll tried to correct the errors of my ways, searching for a way to turn the page.

In recent days I have tried to live right, but trouble seem to follow me wherever I go. Creeping into my day, following into the night, keeping me in it's sight.

Constantly on the run, my mind is ever concerned. There is no freedom for my weary soul, when I'm walking the hills of darkness, through a pass that I have chose.

Only death, will be my freedom. When my eyes will be at rest. Until then, I will be on the outside looking in. listening to the sounds of the howling moon blowing in the wind.

The life I live, I can only do my best. Forever it will be my struggle, nothing gained and nothing less.

My eyes have seen it all. There is a time to rise, and a time to fall, but here and now, I'm left outside the prison wall, yet my soul is at a lost.

"The Trade House Rip Off"

SPARKLES IN THE WINDS

Sparkles in the winds,
with colors from
the rainbow
blending
within.

Golden light splatters
upon the ocean,
and across
the night.

Cascading over rivers and
streams, embellished
with colorful love
Schemes.

A dazzling display,
till the end
of day.

Sparkle in the winds,
when the shooting
stars descend.

Spreading glitter into
the shades of
twilight.

Mystifying the
reasons of
sight.

Sparkles of love takes
full bloom. Blowing
in the wind with
romantic
tunes.

Where the fair winds
blow, over the
mountains and
the valleys
below.

Sun flakes are sprinkled
upon the youth
of daybreak.

Sparkles in the winds,
when the day
comes to
an end.

"Sparkles in the Winds"

THE TOUCH OF MUSIC

I can feel the music touching my soul.
A sensation of love
begin to
unfold.

Spinning in my mind like a carousel.
tugging at my
heart as if a
wishing
well.

It embraces me with pleasure,
emanating a treasure
of colorful sound
waves.

It leads me to dance, and clap
my hands when
the music
play.

I can feel the surge of the melody piercing my heart.
The colorful
harmony
taking
part.

It takes control, I suppose. with
an awesome sound
that gently
flows.

Sharing faded memories of you.
When sunny days
were just
a few.
Bringing them back to view. With lyrics
that paints a
portrait of
you.

It doesn't let me forget,
the wonderful
moments
that we
spent.

Bearing the magic of your misty eyes.
radiating sweet memories
that comes
alive.

To me, that's the way it appears
to be, happening
naturally.

It has been revealed,
harmonizing
with cheer.

"The Touch of Music,"
my heart can feel.

THE ROAR OF THE JAGUAR

The golden sunset had melted into
the tropical night. The myth of a dark
curse hung heavily over a small village,
that rested beneath the eyes of the
moon, glowing with yellowish light.

In the western hemisphere, where
the huge footprints of a killer Jaguar
had been spotted, spread across the
swamps near a poppy field.

The inhabitants of the region were
afraid, as they lay with covers about
their heads, shivering in their beds.

The "Roar of the Jaguar" had been
heard throughout the village.

The native people were of brave
hearts, but on this night the
frightening echo lingered in their
heads, with thought of a man eater
instead.

The Jaguar was cunning, with a
unique style. The stars reflected in his
eyes.

He had a soul of fire, with a burning
desire to survive in the tropical wild.

A visions of yellowish light, that
spurted from his eyes, zoomed in on
his prey from hidden attack sites.

Lurking among the wild trees, in the depths of the wet rainforest, keeping his distance from other prides. His eyes are equipped to see his enemy for miles.

His spotted yellowish and black flamboyant coat is the mark of his glory. He prowls the floor of the rainforest, laying claim to his territory.

Unlike the fast footed Cheetah. This Jaguar had the reputation of being a man eater.

The inhabitants of certain parts of the world, believes that the Jaguar is the god of the underground. Marking his territory as he roams around.

Helping the sun to travel under the earth at night. Ensuring its rising every morning, bringing new light.

In some parts of the world, the Jaguar name means, "a wild beast that kill it's prey with a single bound." Keeping his compact body low to the ground.

He hunts along, in the mountains, rainforest, and swamps. There he makes his home.

Hunting at night, and at times during the day, keeping a steady pace as he stalks his prey.

Dragging the carcasses into trees,
underbrush, and occasionally among
the thick weeds.

Laying low, waiting for prey that's
on the go. With his watchful eyes, as
bright as the sky. He listens for man,
or beast to go by.

Just for the thrill. Men have hunted
this Jaguar with nets and powerful
guns, setting him up for the kill.

Looking for a trophy, or bragging
rights. In a quest to take, "The Roar of
the Jaguar," away from the night.

Hunting man was not in the Jaguar's
plan, but ripping flesh, and spilling
blood is what he understands.

Waiting for the night, to unleash a
fierce fight. Drenched in the tropical
moonlight.

Staying out of sight during the day.
Flaunting colors that blends in with
the scenery, when hunting prey.

Moving swiftly as traveling
underground, never to be found

Keeping a low profile letting no one
get too close, staying in control.

Probing the night air for the scent of
man, or beast. Prowling the rainforest,
and swamps, or where the villagers
have their feast.

Fashioning his hideout among the
enclosure of trees, taking cover amid
the coloration of leaves.

A master of illusion, evading the
danger of intrusion.

In the stillness of a hush, he crouched
within the brush.

The Roar of the Jaguar, warn other
beast to stay away. Roaming the wet
rainforest whether night, or day, in
search of prey.

Fighting to protect his territory,
shining in all his glory.

He's a rare breed, climbing tall trees.
Feeding little cubs, pounding on it's
prey from high above.

Using his sharp teeth, and powerful
jaws, swiftly attacking his prey,
bringing it down with a swipe of his
raze sharp claws.

A symbol of power like roaring
thunder. Said to be the god of the
underworld, roaming down under.

Closely related to the lion, ready to
kill man, or beast at anytime.

Roaming the dense rainforest, leaving
footprints in the sands.

Lurking near streams, and lagoons.
Prowling through the thick
grasslands.

Swimming in the nearby brooks,
resting in high trees. On the lookout
for man, or beast as far as his eye sees.

Once he was captured, by men of evil
intentions never to be mentioned.

He had been chased and encaged,
for several days, but found a way to
escape. A life he would have to take.

Breaking loose, showing proof that
he's the beast of the wild, for the cage
he had no use.

In the wilderness his freedom awaits,
spending time near rivers and lakes.

The mighty Jaguar, man could not
beat. He tramped over them with
huge feet.

His name is believed to have been
derived from the mouth of Indians.
Which means, " he who kills with a
single leap."

Whether in the wet rainforest, or the
mountains afar. Where the fight for
blood and survival occur.

You can hear the Roar of the Jaguar,
roaming the wilderness, competing
with man, beast, and other big cats.
Where the challenges of the wild are
met, with a soul of fire.

"The Roar of the Jaguar"

REFINED BY TIME

Refined by time, like flames
of fire, refining raw gold,
into a value that
never grows
old.

Where strength is
drawn, and
fresh seed
is sown.

I have had good
times. I've
had bad.

What ever I've
had, nothing
seems to
last.

As mystery shape
the pages of
history.

My life is not
a vehicle of
consistency.

I have had what
seemed to
be fun.

Then there are
times when
I had
none.

There were desperate
times, when
I had to
run.

Refined in the
worst of
times.

Refined early in my
prime, feeling as
if I was dying,
when life was
trying

Hardening my
soul and
mind.

Eliminating misery,
that echoes only
in memory.

The drama of life
and death. A
mixture of
old and
new.

Bringing the matters
refined by time.
To me, and to
you, of just
a few.

Sometimes are fitting,
other times I keep
forgetting.

Carrying good
wishes from
the past.

Leaving behind the
wishes that
may not
last.

Your life and mine.
Living in a space,
refined by
time.

WINDMILLS

Windmills, spinning high above the rolling hills. A beautiful sight
from my windowsill,
reaching far across
the open fields.

Turning with the whisper of music, that's cradled in the blending
Winds. Sending energy aid, from
the silver blades, through
the river of shinny days.

Giving magic to the air that leaps to life, from the rotating wheels.
Across the rocky mountains,
to the still valleys, and
the meadows of gold.

Bringing new life into the ages, visible from the endless roads.
Windmill power,
pumping through
the green hours.

Spinning swiftly around, bringing raw energy to the near by towns.
Like the windmills
of our minds, swirls
through the pages of time.

The turbine towers, of robust windmill power. Captures the mighty
wind, as they slowly
spin. Smoothing
out energy spikes.

Throughout the sleepless nights. Round and around they go.
Aligned neatly In a row.
Turning to no end, only
round-and-round again.

Wind on a carousel, with energy and power to share. Extracting
water from deep wells.
Liken to a merry-go-round,
that turns just above the ground.

Beneath the bright sun, bringing cool water that is ready to run.
To meadows and valleys
below, where the wild
flowers blossom and grow.

Windmill towers, triggering primary power. Converging across
the green fields with silver
water wheels. Pumping
energy from across
the rolling hills. For life to live.

"The Swirling Windmills"

SHOOTING FOR STOLEN LOVE

Shooting for Stolen Love,
blazing up the night, like
the shooting stars above.

My love was stolen and
taken away. To get her
back I would have to pay.

Taken on the eve of yesterday.
If this is a game I cannot
afford to play.

The telephone rang, a canary
began to song. Bring money
if you want to see your honey.

Bring gold, for your love has been
stole. Into the night, your love
may be sold to a secret slave site.

Don't summon the cops, we will
make things hot. From the
highest mountaintop, your
love may be dropped.

The crescent moon shined abright.
As I moved through
the city of light.

It was a time for dancing and
Romancing, but on this night,
for my love I must fight.

I'm not a foolish man, I manipulated
their plan. I didn't have money,
but a gun in hand.

I discovered their hideout.
Found my way to the
back door.

Kicked it open then hit the floor.
I used precise timing, my
Adrenalin was climbing.

They had stole my love away.
In due time, they were the one's
who would have to pay.

The men scattered about. I dove into the
place pulling the trigger shooting
the lights out. Pow! Pow!
The gun went loud.

I could hear her scream,
when I burst on the scene.
I was bold, and I was mean.

I found my way into the room,
where she was held captive.
Through an open window came
the light of the moon.

She set along, the love of my own.
drowning in her own tears,
her smile had disappeared.

I released her from the
Chains, that bound her hands
She did not understand,
the scheme of my plan.

I could see the horror on her face.
She came to me with
a thundering embrace.

She appeared as beautiful and
attractive as ever. Only silence
filled the air. My love was in despair.

She spoke to me in a soft voice.
Her lips tried to explain,
she was not to blame.

It seemed strange, that She
was caught up in the
scheme of things.

These men were lurking in the dark.
I knew their names, I thought they
were my friends. That idea was
gone with the wind.

Right from the start,
they tried to keep us apart.

Passing themselves off as
someone who cared.

Their concern must have gone.
Their hearts were filled
with dead men bones

My love and I escaped with glee.
If our hearts would allow, we
would keep a low profile.

Shooting for Stolen Love,
beneath The falling stars above.

The stars in the sky,
give magic to our eyes.
Keeping our dreams alive.

I roamed the night, and roamed
the day. In search of my
stolen love, as a tiger
for it's prey.

From dawn to dusk, fighting
for the sweet love
that belong to us.

Her eyes now sparkle like the
rising sun. the danger of
my job is done.

My love is alive, like the
stars above, that zoom
across the sky.

"Shooting for Stolen Love"

THE DREAMER

The Dreamer, envisioning scenery
that his eyes have never seen.

Places his mind has spent, but his
body has never went.

Places his eyes long to see.
Somewhere he is dreaming to be.

Into his conscious he has journeyed
to wonderful places. Traveled to
oasis's, a rich lifestyle his heart
chases.

Through the eyes of his mind he can
see the exotic sights, that glows in
the Polynesian nights.

Hear the sound of fresh new music
that have never been heard before.
Coming from an invisible door.

Drifting in the pleasure center of his
mind, out of the motion pictures of
time.

Taken to the winds, where the
desires of his heart have been.

Silver and gold, he dreams of the
day his hand will hold.

Sailing around the world, in
possession of diamonds and pearls.

In the afternoon, spanning beyond
the midnight moon, he dreams.

Staring into the sunset, toward the
early morning sunrise. Behold the
dreams that glows within his eyes.

He has not demonstrated shiny
talent, athletic skills, or a brilliant
mind.

He dream of the day he will find.
Nevertheless, whatever he endeavors
he dreams of being the best.

He dream of gorgeous colors, giving
his woman a gift of fur mink, not
white, nor brown, but pretty-in-
pink.

Attending far away shows, where
treasures glitter with pure gold.

Where days are full of endless
wonder of delight, sailing across the
magnificent nights.

Images flows through his mind, like
rays of sunshine.

Colorful pictures emanate in his
imagination as stars of the milky
ways, enlightening his days.

Dreams of new love, holding hands,
and playing in the sand has never
came, but his hope still remain.
New found love, from the heavens
above.

Dreams of summertime fun, in
places where he use to run.

His dreams may seem to be in vain,
but they ease a heart of pain.

Dreams of portraits comes alive in
the world of his imagination. Like
golden sunlight, beaming across the
night.

Painting the valleys below, with
colors from beyond the rainbow.

Beautiful swans that bring music to
the wind, then take to the air again.

Gazing upon the blue skies, with
dreams in his eyes. Listening to the
magic of sound, watching the sun
go down.

Radiant light, shining bright, in a
beamier. He constantly stares into
the night.

"The Dreamer"

TIME WAITS NOT

Time waits not, a wise
man once
revealed.

'In this life you only
get one shot.
There is no
time to
kill.'

Time waits for no one,
beneath the blazing
sun. An early
lesson one
must learn.

It gravitate with speed.
Leaving only shades
of memories,
and fading
deeds.

Once time was on my
side. Suddenly it
seems to have
passed me
by.

My soul is running
with the wind.
Trying to
catch up
again.

It fads away like the evening
sun. perhaps vanishing
into the hollow sky,
as if it has
wings to
fly.

Fast as it go, I have
nothing to
show.

Time was once before
my eyes. When I
was running
wild.

Now it seems to
have brushed
right by.

Gone with the winds,
that carried
the winters
away.

Gone with the cold days.
For the waste of
time, my soul
pays.

Time waits not. If
living unwise,
it takes what
you've
got.

It carried away the
love my heart
held so
dear.

Carried away the happy
days, that filled
my heart with
cheer.

Leaving behind a little
quiet time, that
I may find, to
ease my
mind.

Framing memories of
the good times,
that I once
had.

Hanging fading
pictures in
the past.

Recalling precious
moments that
could not
last.

Time waits not.
Give thanks
for what
you've
got.